UNDER ONE ROOF

UNDER ONE ROOF

HOW A TOUGH OLD WOMAN IN A LITTLE OLD HOUSE CHANGED MY LIFE

BARRY MARTIN
WITH
PHILIP LERMAN

HarperCollins*Publishers*

HarperCollins*Publishers*
77–85 Fulham Palace Road,
Hammersmith, London W6 8JB

www.harpercollins.co.uk

First published in the US by St Martin's Press 2013
This UK edition published by HarperCollins*Publishers* 2014

1 3 5 7 9 10 8 6 4 2

Design by Phil Mazzone

A catalogue record of this book
is available from the British Library

ISBN 978-0-00-754302-1

Printed and bound in Great Britain by
Clays Ltd, St Ives plc

MIX
Paper from
responsible sources
FSC® C007454

For Edith
and for my dad,
William M. Martin Jr.

UNDER ONE ROOF

1

I finally moved the cookies.

They were Walkers Pure Butter Shortbread cookies, the only brand of cookies Edith liked. They came from Scotland, and when you would eat them it was like you just ate a tab of butter. I remember she sent me to the store for cookies once, and they didn't have her brand, so I brought not one, not two, but three others home. She took a bite of each one, and pushed them back at me. "All yours," she snapped, staring up at me with those piercing blue eyes. "Not mine."

It was always a battle of wills with Edith.

I eventually hunted down the Walkers at the old Ballard market. When I brought them home, she took one bite and said, "Well, that was worth waiting for, don't you think?" Like she was a schoolteacher who'd just taught her problem student a simple lesson. There I was, a fifty-year-old man, a person with a position of responsibility, and she still made me feel like a kid, every single time.

After she died, and for the longest time after that, I couldn't touch anything in her house. Like that box of cookies. It just sat there on the shelf next to the stove in that cramped kitchen, staring down at me, as if it was daring me to throw it out. Like it knew I wouldn't. I was going to take the cookies over to the trailer at the construction site and let the boys have them. I brought the box to the door twice, at least, and set it down, and thought, well, I'll get it when I go out. But when I was leaving, I just couldn't take the cookies. I couldn't leave them sitting by the door, either, because Edith would hate it if anything was out of place. So I'd pick them up and put them back on the shelf, right where they belonged, lengthwise, with the name "Walkers" showing on a bed of Scottish plaid.

I guess I just wasn't ready.

I'm sitting in her house right now for what will probably be the last time, and looking at all this stuff, and wondering why it has such an effect on me. For the last couple of months, I've come over here, trying to pack up her things. There's just so much. The music alone is going to take half a day. There's the albums, hundreds of them: Mantovani, for example. Maybe thirty of those. Who the heck has thirty Mantovani albums? And tons of Guy Lombardo. Then all these cassettes on the wall, in a cheap little wooden cassette case that's sagging in the middle—cassettes of Caruso and Beethoven and Benny Goodman. And CDs. Hundreds and hundreds of CDs. I guess she moved along with the times, up to a point—the albums, then the cassettes, then the CDs. The progression stops there, but still, it's kind of funny to see so many CDs in a house where everything else feels like it's straight out of the fifties. Anyway, I'd come here to pack stuff up, then walk around in circles for fifteen minutes, and leave without touching anything.

Even after all this time, whenever I walk in that front door, I expect to see her lying on the couch. I haven't sat on that couch even once—I can't bring myself to sit on it, the couch she lay on every day and slept on every night. I think I haven't moved anything because she was just so particular that everything went back exactly where it was. There are hundreds of little ceramic figurines all over this place—lots of cows, and some little dogs and cats. She loved animals: here's a ceramic cat at a piano that says "Meow-sic" and a begging dog and a bunch of little ceramic pigs. And back in the kitchen, she had the figurines from the Red Rose tea boxes. I don't think she even liked the tea all that much, but she loved those little figurines. I read somewhere that Red Rose has given away 300 million of those little toy statues. Sometimes it feels like Edith had half of them.

And if you moved any of her figurines, anywhere in the house, she'd notice and get heartburn. One time my wife and daughter came down here to clean up the house a little, and the next day Edith was so irritated. "Where's this?" and "What's that doing over there?" she said to me. I asked her, what does it matter, but that just made her more irritated because she wanted things where they belonged. Maybe it's because that's where her mother kept things. Edith had a really strong connection with her mother, and a lot of things changed when her mother died. Or I guess it's more accurate to say, a lot of things had to stay the same.

I think a lot of people face this when their parent dies. Edith wasn't my mother, of course, and in a lot of ways I felt more like a parent to her, taking care of her like she was a child, not to put too fine a point on it. I still faced those same issues, though. The difficulty of accepting that she's really gone. You question yourself: Did I do everything I was supposed to do? I think that until you answer that question, you can't accept what's happened. Maybe that's why I kept everything just where it was, like in a state of suspended animation, while I thought about it.

It was such a strange turn of events that brought me into this little house. There I was, just going to work every day, a project superintendent in charge of building a shopping mall on a lot that was empty except for this one little ramshackle house we had to build around. It wasn't my fault that there was this struggle between the project and this lady's house. It's just the job. The developers were trying to get her to move. She was digging in her heels, insisting that she was going to stay. And there was me, caught in the middle. Everyone thought I was trying to trick her into moving. But the truth was just the opposite. I was doing everything I could to allow her to stay.

So what, you might ask, was I doing over there? What was in it for me?

Good question.

I guess, if you try to dissect the friendship that formed between us—and a lot of people seem to want to do that—you could start with the books.

Over on one wall, next to the couch, there was a whole collection of classic books, like *Wuthering Heights* and *Canterbury Tales* and *Das Kapital* and the poems of Longfellow. They were all dusty, like no one had read them for a long time, but every once in a while she'd quote from them, so I know she read them all, some more than once.

I think that's one of the things that drew me in. I was fascinated with how much she knew. I guess that's because I never met anyone who had read as much, who knew as much, as Edith did. It was like meeting someone from another planet. A different kind of intelligence. It just draws you in.

And then, of course, there were the stories. Edith's stories.

For a guy like me, growing up like I did, you didn't exactly run into people every day who told you they were Benny Goodman's cousin. Or who taught Mickey Rooney some dance steps. Or escaped a Nazi concentration camp. Or said they did, anyway.

Here's exactly what I thought of that, at first:

Wack job.

Not very nice, I know. But that's where I was at, pure and simple.

But as I started to go over there more often, and heard more and more of the stories—just little bits and pieces of them, just enough to make you wonder—I found myself wanting to hear more. Looking at Edith was a little like looking at those books: a million stories hidden in there. Maybe half of her stories weren't true. But it was real interesting, just to know they were there.

I was never much of a reader, myself. There weren't a

whole lot of books around my house, growing up. I guess if I was going to school today they would have diagnosed me with attention deficit disorder, because I could never really focus on reading or anything like that. But as it was, I muddled through. I never even watched a lot of movies, to tell you the truth. Take me to a movie theater and I'd be asleep in fifteen minutes. Just couldn't focus on it. But I did watch a few movies with Edith. She had tons of tapes all around this room as well, all movies from the forties and fifties. Lots of Bette Davis, lots of Sherlock Holmes. A lot of Greta Garbo, too: *Grand Hotel*, *Anna Christie*, *Ninotchka*. Somebody told me they thought Edith was a little like Garbo, holed up here in this little 106-year-old house in a shabby section of Seattle—but they had it wrong.

Edith didn't want to be alone.

2

I was nervous, that first day on the job, walking up to her house. I'd heard so much already. At first I hadn't been paying too much attention. I'm not that much of a reader, as I mentioned, and I hadn't seen any of the articles in the paper, or heard about how the local newspaper reporters were all scared of Edith because she'd chase them away whenever they got within ten feet of her. In fact, when I got the job as construction superintendent for the shopping mall project, my wife asked me, "Oh, is that the one where the old lady won't move?" And I said no, because I was sure I would have heard about it.

But when I mentioned it to the guys I worked for, they told me that yes, they had this stubborn old lady, like a little bulldog with wire-framed glasses, holding up the whole works. They'd gotten every other inch of the property they wanted, basically a city block square, except for this one little ramshackle house. Now they were having to build around it.

And if anyone tried to talk to her, she'd more likely bite their head off than give them the time of day.

The first time I looked at the architect's drawing, I saw the tiny rectangle that was cut out where Edith's house stood. Later, the owners of the project and I talked it over, and we decided to put some steel embeds in the side walls facing Edith's house, big galvanized steel plates with metal studs that go back and tie into the concrete. If she wound up selling, we could tear down her house and build across by welding beams to those embeds—basically filling in the little rectangle. And if she didn't, well, I had perfectly good plans for building around her. To me, it was a construction job, and a pretty big one at that. I didn't really care one way or the other.

The wheels had all got set in motion about a year earlier, back in the spring of 2005. I had worked for one construction company for almost ten years. For a while, there was a ton of work. Up here in Seattle, we really reaped the benefit of the dot-com boom even more than people know. I was a project superintendent, meaning I was basically in charge of all the people and subcontractors on a big project, such as an office building. It was the kind of thing that you figured, well, this is what my life is gonna be, and I'll retire with this company. And you feel pretty good about it.

Then the dot-coms all went down and things got strange. There was a glut of office space, so the banks started pulling the plug on any project with office space in it. There just wasn't enough work to go around. The company I worked for finally went out of business. I went to work for another fellow, building assisted-living facilities.

I wouldn't know until later how ironic that was. When it became my whole life's work just to keep one old lady out of them.

The boss was a good person to work for; the firm was small, and I was given a lot of autonomy, so it was easy to get things done. I was happy just to have landed on my feet, given how tough things were. But that spring, all the guys from my old company, the one that went out of business, got involved with another firm, called Ledcor. The owner of the old company came to run Ledcor's Seattle office, and the old operations manager came on board, and the business-development guy, and their best project manager. Then they called me to come join the party.

I loved working with that crew. They were nice guys, and they really cared about you. They had this project they wanted me to do, and—not to put too fine a point on it—they started hounding me. Hounding me in a nice way, of course. But I knew what they were doing. The first calls came from the project manager, a great guy named Roger Wagner. Roger wouldn't tell me too much about the job—just that it involved a whole city block, and that once that was done, there were one or two other blocks, and by the way, this Ledcor was a great place to work.

See, that's how it works: he's sticking the bait out there and waiting to see how hard you're sniffing. Then if you're interested, he'll feed you the bait and reel you in. I knew what he was doing—and he knew that I knew—so it was all very jovial. But at the same time, I was a little intrigued, because you never know what's going to happen tomorrow so you never slam the door on anything.

The next one to call me was the operations manager. He was also giving it the soft sell, because nobody wanted to seem too eager. So we all went around it for a month or two, until they finally gave me the are-you-in-or-are-you-out call.

It was a tough decision. These guys were like family to me, but I hated leaving the job I had. I don't like leaving things without a reason. I need to be able to say, well, this bothers me or that bugs me. But there was nothing wrong with where I was. I looked for a reason to justify the move, and all I could come up with was, well, these guys have a better retirement program or a better bonus-potential program, or they're large enough that there is room for me to grow. But I knew that at that point I was just making excuses to do what I already knew I wanted to do.

So I said, I'm in.

The project was to build a shopping mall. A developer, the Bridge Group, had purchased most of a city block in Ballard, a nice, sleepy waterfront neighborhood just over a short bridge from downtown Seattle. But the project got stalled off just as I came on board, so they had me working on another project in the meantime. That Christmas, while I was still waiting to get started down in Ballard, a columnist for *The Seattle Times* apparently wrote about an odd phenomenon that went on down near the site. I didn't read about it at the time, but I heard about it later: At night, after the bars closed, lots of people with no place else to go would park their cars on the side streets, and kind of live in them. The columnist, a guy named Danny Westneat, wrote that one night he counted forty-one live-in vehicles parked in a couple-block area—right in the neighborhood where I was going to be building the mall.

In the article he quoted Edith, saying she thought that maybe two hundred or three hundred of these itinerants camped out in this rolling car colony on the weekends. You'd think the locals would be pretty furious that the cops were letting this go on, but her attitude was "What can you do? They don't have any money, so where can they go? The way I see it, if they don't bother me, I don't bother them." Seemed like a pretty philosophical approach. I didn't see that article until much later, but when somebody did show it to me, I was kind of surprised—you don't expect someone with a reputation for being so ornery and crotchety to be so accepting of stuff like that.

Sometimes people aren't who you think they are.

It was spring of 2006 when most of the permits cleared and we could finally get rolling. I got down there early that first day, to do what I always do when I start a job. I began by going around to all the neighbors on the surrounding streets, introducing myself to people, making sure they had my cell phone number in case there were any problems. I always feel like it's good to get that up front first. You can't pretend to do a big job like this right down the block from someone and not have them notice, or act like you're never gonna cause them a problem. But you can let them know you care enough to hear about what you're doing that's annoying folks, and you're willing to meet them halfway. I feel like it's my responsibility. If someone was doing that to me, I'd expect the same.

The first day of breaking ground still gets to me after all these years of working construction. It's that sense of anticipation you feel on the first day of school—excited and nervous all at the same time. Especially when you break ground in springtime. There's something about that fresh spring air that gets in your blood, and it was getting to me as I walked the streets of Ballard that morning, although, to be honest, Edith's block was no bed of roses. Her street still had a lot of those transients living in cars, and you could see a few of them sleeping in their dilapidated old vehicles that morning. They had a tendency to clean out the nearby Dumpsters and then toss whatever garbage they had right outside the cars, and use the weeds for their Porta-Potty, so it wasn't the most savory atmosphere you could imagine. Pretty disgusting, actually.

But as I approached Edith's house, I got a strong whiff of fresh-mown grass, and it took me back to when I was a kid, mowing lawns for quarters. Same thing happens to me in the fall, the smell of leaves and the snap in the air. It takes me back to when I'd go hunting with my dad. Those smells bring you back to happy times, and they kind of bring the happiness back with them. It's a good feeling.

In the springtime I always think I'm smelling the bubble gum that came with baseball cards. I was probably imagining things, but that's what it felt like as I approached Edith's front gate. For just a moment, you feel like a man and a child all at the same time.

Most of the sidewalk on Edith's block is overgrown with blackberry bushes, but they stop at her property line. Her yard is like a little clearing in that jungle. Within that clearing, Edith's house looks like something out of a storybook. A compact building, two floors, plus a basement that peeks up out of the ground, the whole thing maybe twenty feet wide. It's set about ten feet back from the sidewalk and the ground slopes down toward the house so the foundation is a good three feet lower than the street in front of it, making the house seem even smaller than it is. Or as if the house is crouching a few feet from the street, tired from too many years of trying to stand up straight.

There's a tiny entranceway in front, with an arched opening. It looks like the miniature house on the front of a Swiss cuckoo clock, and you half expect a little wooden soldier to come sliding out of it every hour on the hour. There's a small patch of grass, which Edith kept neat and tidy. It's somewhat overgrown with dandelions now, but when I first walked past the house, it was one of the first things I noticed: how tidy the lawn was. It brightened up the neighborhood: a beautiful oasis in that ugly place, with irises planted all around it. It felt welcoming, and drew your eye away from all that urban decay. It made me feel good to see someone who, from outside appearances anyway, was happy with how she had things, especially when what she had wasn't much. Most people complain about what they don't have; here was someone making the most of what she did have.

Edith was tending her garden that morning. Kneeling down like that, it looked like she was praying, or looking for something she'd lost. My first reaction was one of relief. She reminded me of my great-grandma, a small, sweet, meek-looking lady, like someone in a storybook who would have a mouse for a pet. I was still a little leery, though, because I didn't know how she was handling the news about the construction, and because of what the guys had told me about her.

"Hi, I'm Barry Martin," I said. "I'm going to be building this project around you." I braced for the worst.

"Well, I'm pleased to meet you," she said, rising slowly, like she was unfolding her limbs one by one. "I'm Edith Wilson Macefield."

A concrete truck from the Salmon Bay Concrete Plant a half-block down from her house roared past us, keeping us from talking for a moment. We sized each other up in silence, waiting for the truck to pass. Even standing up, Edith was a little stooped over, with a hunch to her back, and hazel-blue eyes that didn't quite both look at you at the same time. She had to pick one eye to fix on you, but she made up for it by looking at you straight and hard, and not letting go of your gaze once she had it. She was a thin woman with white hair and a wide face, and looked like the kind of person who cared more about her appearance than you might expect of someone that age, especially someone seemingly so isolated. She was wearing a blue knit sweater and a pair of slacks and some garden gloves, and she pulled off one glove, walked over, and shook my hand. Even though she was small and frail, her handshake seemed strong and confident. I was relieved—the anger I'd expected from her hadn't materialized. But I felt a little sad, too, to see this old woman, apparently living so alone.

"Well, nice to meet you, Miss Macefield," I said. The concrete truck had passed, and the rumble of cars coming over the bridge had stopped for the moment; all of a sudden the air was still and silent, the way it gets on a warm spring day. You could hear someone mowing a lawn a few blocks away, it was that quiet.

I had introduced myself to just about everybody who would be affected by the project, but as much as I knew this was all just part of the job, this particular introduction seemed different—I mean, we were going to build a shopping mall all around this lady's house. I couldn't imagine what that would be like. Or actually, I could. A hell of a lot of noise and dirt and debris and destruction. I had the urge to sugarcoat it a bit, to try to make it seem less disturbing than it was likely to be; but one look at Edith and you knew: this was not a lady who took her medicine with a spoonful of sugar.

"Miss Macefield, I just want to let you know we're going to be making a whole lot of noise and creating a big mess. There's no way around that. But if you ever need anything, or have any problems, here's my number. Don't hesitate to call."

"Well, that's very nice of you," she said, taking my card, holding it up close to one eye, then tucking it into a front pocket of her slacks. "I'm glad to have you here. It'll be nice to have a little company."

As we talked, she picked up a bag of birdseed and started spreading it on the sidewalk.

"Like to feed the birds, do you?" I asked.

"Every morning," she replied. "I'm running late today. Had a little trouble with insomnia last night, so then I fell asleep and woke up a little late."

"Well," I said, "let us know if you need anything."

"Thank you," she said, and then, as I walked away, I heard over my shoulder: "You can call me Edith."

I heard the rumble of the cars across the bridge nearby. I thought I got a whiff of that baseball-card bubble gum, too. I looked back and saw Edith struggle to get down to her knees, until her whole form was tucked behind the chain-link fence that faced her house, as though she had revealed just a little bit of herself, just for a moment, and now she was going back into hiding.

It's funny how the most momentous conversations of your life—or the ones that turn out to be the most momentous— can seem, in the moment they happen, so mundane.

I stopped one more time and turned back to look at the house, standing lonely and deserted on that broken-down street. It seemed impossible, but the developers had already offered Edith $750,000. Three quarters of a million dollars, probably ten times what the house was worth—and she turned them down cold. I guess I should have known going into it that I would run into people who would give me a hard time, building a big, hulking mall around that tiny house. The other side of town—if you looked to the left of the Ballard Bridge as you crossed into town, instead of to the right toward Edith's house—was already the site of a lot of new develop- ment, development that many people thought was killing the character of good old Ballard. And the deals had been closed to build a whole lot more. Because Edith's was the last house standing on her block, people saw her as a symbol, a force against "yuppification," against the overdevelopment of old neighborhoods with character and charm. I was the man bringing in change, she was the woman who wanted things to stay the same. That same *Seattle Times* columnist who wrote the story about the homeless people, Danny Westneat, had also written a column in February about Edith's so-called last stand. A few days later, he wrote about how that column had "unwittingly unearthed an entire community of folks who have been captivated by her for years." He quoted one resident as saying, "I salute her for standing up to some of the 'progress' that's coming to Ballard." Another one wrote, "I've come to love this lady, and I don't even know her."

Someone in the office showed me the article, and when I read it over, I was struck by the ending of it, what the guy wrote about Edith. He said, "How she lives and the choice she made to stay put seems to spark powerful feelings in total strangers. It did me, yet I've spoken to her only three times. I think it's because she's genuine. Authentic. She's living the life she's got and not asking for help, pity or money.

"What does it say about us," Danny wrote, "that we find that so remarkable?"

As the days went by, I didn't have occasion to talk to Edith again, but I noticed that the birdseed was, indeed, out on the sidewalk almost every day before we got to work. It was funny, but all the guys started watching out for it—and for her. After a while, if the birdseed wasn't out by 10:30 or 11:00 a.m., somebody would let me know. The first time, I didn't think much of it, but the second or third time, I decided I'd better go over and check on her.

I knocked on the door.

"Go away!" I heard her shout from inside. "Leave me alone!"

I was stunned. I was sure she'd change her tune when she realized it was friendly old me.

The rumble from the bridge had quieted down. The wind had kicked up, though, and nearly blew my baseball cap off my head. I tried again. "Edith," I said, "it's me, Barry, from the construction site. I just wanted to make sure you're okay."

"Are you deaf?" she yelled. "I said go away! Leave me alone!"

I thought, well, okay, this is what everybody told me to expect. Shouldn't be surprised.

"Well, just glad to know you're okay," I called in, making one more attempt to rescue this conversation, if you could call it that. "Let us know if you need anything."

I guess that insulted her, like I was saying she couldn't take care of herself. "I'm fine! Go away!"

I walked back over to our construction trailer, scratching my head. Was it something I said? It's pretty hard to mess up "Hello," though. Once again, I felt like a little kid who'd gotten yelled at by the teacher.

I got the same response the next few times I went over to check on her, over the next couple of weeks, trying to get a look inside and make sure she was okay. Maybe I should have been offended or pissed off by that, but to tell you the truth, I really just felt kind of sad for her. I figured maybe she wasn't feeling so well, and there she was all alone. I also felt kind of embarrassed—I don't even know the woman, and here I am, popping open her mail slot and peeping inside.

I started to wonder if maybe there weren't two sides to Edith: the polite, gracious, friendly side, accepting of the change all around her; and the cranky, crotchety side, quick to anger and to take offense. And I thought, maybe there was a reason for that. The first time I went over, I treated Edith with dignity and respect, and she reacted the same way— pleasant and courteous. But maybe she didn't like it if she thought people were checking up on her; she didn't like what that implied, which was that she couldn't take care of herself. I think that's what happens when people get older. They know a time is coming when they won't be able to take care of themselves, and they're fighting it. They don't want to admit what's happening and it makes them mad when you remind them. That's the first lesson that Edith taught me, and I didn't know it then, but it would be the first of many. For the time that I knew her, Edith's little house would become my school-house. She taught me about what I guess they call the conti-nuity of things—what we learn from the older generation and what we pass along.

I met Edith just in time, it turns out. My dad was seventy-three years old, and holding up pretty well so far, but soon enough he'd start having his own problems. I think if it weren't for the things I started learning from Edith, I wouldn't have known how to handle or accept what was happening to my father. Or how to help him.

But for the moment, I put those thoughts aside. Everybody's got their problems. I had plenty of my own.

I had a shopping mall to build.

3

There's a lot of sitting-around time at the beginning of a project, especially one like this that begins with tearing down buildings to make way for the new construction. There were two buildings on the other end of the lot from where Edith's house stood that we had to get rid of. I'd given the crew their assignments, and now the best thing for me to do was stay the heck out of their way and let them do their jobs. So I found myself wandering from my trailer over to Edith's front gate, not forty feet away. Now that I'd figured out what pushed her buttons—or thought I'd figured it out, anyway—I started approaching her a little differently. I only went over when I saw her outside, when it didn't seem like I was checking up on her. And I kept it casual, chatting about the weather and the transients and whatnot. Pretty soon we were hanging on the fence like any neighbors, poking fun at the way teenagers dress these days, what we recalled about Ballard years ago, trying to remember the names of who ran which store, that sort of thing.

As we talked, day by day, little bits of her past would seep into the conversation. Once we were talking about something we'd heard on the radio, another dumb government botch-up. "It's not just here, believe me. When I worked for the British government, let me tell you, there were some royal mess-ups there as well." A van turned off the overpass and drove by with its muffler roaring; I had to wait for it to pass before I could ask, "You worked for the British government, Edith?"

"Yes," she said, without missing a beat. "It's how I wound up in the concentration camp in Dachau."

Well, that threw me for a loop. I wanted to ask her about it, but before I could say any more, I saw that her eyes were moist, that tears were starting to form. I had this overwhelming feeling like I wanted to hug her, but of course I didn't. I realized why I was feeling it, though. Because in that moment, looking at Edith, I felt like I was back in the presence of someone I loved as much as I've ever loved anyone: my great-grandma Mimi.

I flashed back on the time when I graduated from eighth grade, and my sister was graduating from high school. My dad rented a 35-foot cabin cruiser. The whole family, including my great-grandmother, went on the boat and cruised through the Canadian San Juan Islands for a week. That trip made a real impression on me. I loved watching my dad steer that boat. He was so smooth and confident and in control, it made me feel really safe on the water. I still carry that with me.

And I loved having all that time with Great-grandma Mimi. I could sit and listen to her tell stories all day. Great-grandma Mimi came to Washington State in a covered wagon. A covered wagon! I could just see her—in a kid's mind, of course, your great-grandmother is always an old lady—but I'd try to picture her as a young woman, and as she'd tell me her stories, I'd imagine what it must have been like at those moments of her life—when she first heard a radio, when she first got a telephone. She was there when the automobile was invented, when men went off to the First World War, and when they came home. And there I was, just a kid cruising on the open sea between beautiful islands, the cool Canadian breezes giving you a little chill, even on a summer's morning, the sun gleaming off pristine green waters, and my great-grandmother Mimi touching my cheek and telling me what it was like the first time she heard a phonograph.

A few years back, I was talking with my kids about the moon landing. It was the fortieth anniversary or something like that, and it was all over the TV, and they were asking me about it, and I told them to try to imagine what it was like for my great-grandmother that day. She came to Washington State in a covered wagon, and now she was watching a man walk on the moon. That's really something. I know people talk about all the technological advances we have today, with computers and all, but to me it's nothing compared with what my great-grandmother lived through. The changes she saw unfolding around her.

I looked over at Edith. She had turned her back to me; to

gain her composure, I thought. But then I noticed a little dog in her yard, and Edith was walking toward it.

It was a cute dog, one of those Lhasa Apsos, only about seventeen years old, missing most of its teeth, and blind as a bat. It was a stubborn little dog, too. There was a cart out in the front yard, and the dog was walking along and, because it was so blind, it bonked into the cart. Instead of going around it, the dog just walked forward and bonked its head on the cart again, over and over. It would be a while before I figured out that the dog had got its stubborn streak from its owner.

"What's your dog's name, Edith?"

"Oh, that's Mimi," she said. "Mimi's been with me forever."

"You're kidding! That's was my great-grandma's name. Mimi."

Edith smiled. She seemed to take some kind of special pleasure in that coincidence.

For the next hour or so, we chatted about nothing. Edith wanted to know all about my family: my son, Willy, who was sixteen, pitching and playing middle infield for the baseball team; and my daughter, Kelsey, a year older, who was into what they call competitive cheerleading. I would never in a million years have heard of competitive cheerleading if my kid hadn't been into it, but now I was becoming something of an expert. And of course my wife, Evie, the one who holds us all together.

When I mentioned Evie's name, Edith's eyes opened wide. "That's just quite remarkable," she said. "One of my best friends was named Evelyn. We called her Evie, too. One of my best friends in the world. That was back in England, of course. Those were some days we had, Evelyn and myself."

It all started to make sense, in a way. I hadn't put two and two together the first time she mentioned she worked for the British government, but from the way she spoke, not with an accent but with such precise and unusual diction, you could guess that maybe she had lived somewhere else for a long time. "When did you live in England, Edith?" I asked.

"Yes, yes," she said, not really answering my question. "I haven't thought about Evelyn in a long time. You know, these kinds of connections are important. People think they aren't, but they really are."

It was comforting, in a way, hearing Edith talk like this. A little like being back with Great-grandma Mimi. I didn't feel right then that I could ask Edith any more about Britain and Germany and all that, but I knew it would come up again. I got a little bit of the thrill of anticipation: I couldn't wait to hear more of her stories.

I suppose it had been a long time since anyone had hung around Edith's fence just to pass the time of day. I think maybe when you get old, people make assumptions about you—that you're crochety, or solitary, or that you don't want to talk to people—and then those assumptions get in the way. In Edith's case, I guess she'd given people lots of reasons to make those assumptions—but still, as I got to talking with her, I realized that there was a lot more to her than just that. Maybe it was just like the mall project that was taking shape behind her house: in spending afternoons talking the way we had, we managed to clear away some old obstacles, to break some new ground. It was a nice feeling. Like starting out on a long walk, and knowing you're headed in the right direction.

Maybe it was because of all that, or maybe not, but about 10:30 one morning, my cell phone rang.

"Hello, Barry? Is that you?" I didn't know the number, but I recognized the voice right away.

"Morning, Edith. This is Barry. Everything okay?"

"Why yes, Barry, everything is fine. Thank you so much for asking."

There was a long pause. I had the feeling she was searching for the right words, so I just held tight and waited.

"I would like to ask you something," she finally said. "I don't feel comfortable driving today. I was wondering if you might drive me to my hair appointment. I'd certainly understand if it's too much trouble, of course. I know you're a very busy man. I certainly don't want to be a bother."

I was surprised at the request, because I already had figured out that she valued her independence above just about anything else. Like when I'd go check on her, I had to make it look like I was just happening by, or she'd get angry. Edith seemed like the kind of person who didn't like you to do things for them—or didn't want to appear to be asking, anyway. So that's why the call kind of caught me off guard. Still, it was almost a relief to me, because every time I saw her get in the car to drive, I had the sense that the opportunity for an accident was pretty high.

"Sure thing, Edith. No problem. What time?"

"The appointment is at one thirty," she said. "Perhaps you could meet me at a quarter after."

"Not a problem," I said a second time. "I'll meet you by the car. See you then."

"Thank you," she said, slowly and sincerely. "That's very kind."

A few minutes later I told my project manager, Roger, why I'd be gone for a little while that afternoon. No sooner were the words out of my mouth than he started giving me the business. "Hey, so you're going to be driving Miss Daisy, huh? Well, I'm gonna have to record this moment for posterity."

At a quarter after one, I was out in front of Edith's house, standing next to her 1989 blue Chevy Cavalier. It was a sturdy little car, with a dent in the right front fender. She'd inherited it from a friend she had taken care of; she'd helped him through his dying months, and when he passed, he left her all his stuff, including the car.

As I helped Edith into the car, there was Roger, grinning from ear to ear, snapping away with a little digital camera. He was being polite about it, so as not to embarrass Edith, but after I got her into the car and was walking around to the driver's side, he started in again: "Have fun driving Miss Daisy," he said under his breath. Funny, I had never seen that movie, and wouldn't wind up seeing it for a couple of years, but when I did, I couldn't believe how much of that movie we had lived, Edith and me.

I could have taken my truck, but I just thought it would be hard for her to climb up into the cab. Still, it was a bit odd, getting into her car, she had a kind of straw booster seat on the driver's side; I guess it was the only way she could see over the steering wheel. I had just about sat down when I hit my head on the inside of the roof, and I had to wiggle myself back out and move that booster seat into the back. Edith looked over and laughed.

"I guess you're just a little bit bigger than me," she said.

"Yeah, well, getting a little wider every year, too," I said.

On the way to the hairdresser's, Edith and I started talking about how much we liked Ballard. It still says Seattle on the map, but Ballard's always been a world unto itself. It used to be more of an industrial enclave, although one with a real neighborhood feel; the industry and the residents fit together like a hand and a soft old glove. It had become kind of seedy and run-down over the last couple of years, but it still had the feeling of a community of people who cared about one another. The old Ballard crowd seemed to have known one another for a million years, Edith included. And run-down though the neighborhood might be, they were pretty united against the yuppie paradise that they thought Ballard was becoming, now that the development had begun.

I guess I could see their point, in a way, although I had to admit that the development was helping put food on my table, so I couldn't complain too much.

We drove under the ramp of the bridge that goes over the ship canal, which connects Puget Sound to Lake Washington. The bridge itself connects Ballard to Seattle proper, and it's central to everything that happened. At some point, people started realizing what a great place this would be to live—right on the water and, thanks to that bridge, such an easy commute to downtown. Only the folks who already lived here didn't see it that way. They saw this all as an invasion. Edith and I were driving past a few of the new condos that were going up, the ones that all the Old Ballard folks were all upset about.

For a while, the condos were popping up like popcorn. At one point, in fact, they put a moratorium on residential construction and set aside five thousand acres for industrial use, because all of the industry was getting pushed out and everybody was up in arms about losing the heart and soul of Old Ballard. Most of the condos that had gone up so far were actually a little ways to the south, and I was surprised, at first, that the developers were putting up a shopping mall here on Edith's block, because I didn't think there were enough people to warrant it. But when I heard about all the new condos that were planned, the project seemed more like a no-brainer.

On the opposite side of the canal was the spot where they park the boats for the TV show *Deadliest Catch*. You couldn't quite see it from where we were driving, but I'd passed it earlier and seen a tour group forming on the dock. I mentioned it to Edith, and commented on how much Ballard had changed since the last time I'd been here, which had been a while ago. I'd come down to go to the locks and walk around, and there was a construction supply place I used to go to every once in a while. We were just down the road from that place now. I asked Edith if all of the change that was coming to Ballard bothered her the way it did some people.

"No, it doesn't really matter," Edith said. "Change is change. You know, that building you're going to build, twenty years from now they'll tear that down, too. They tore down the Kingdome, just twenty-five years after they built it, you know. They still owed twenty million dollars on it. That's just progress, Barry. That's just how things go."

"Well, that's pretty philosophical of you, Edith," I said.

"Not philosophical at all," she said. "Realistic. World of difference between the two. Things are what they are."

I wondered what it was in her life that made her so accepting of change, and at the same time so stubborn about it when she wanted to be.

As we drove, I mentioned that I heard they were thinking of tearing down the Denny's that had been a fixture in the town since the sixties. I'd been driving past that Denny's every morning on my way to work.

"Well, the plans are all messed up," Edith said. "Some folks are trying to get historical status for it. You know those big, sweeping beams it has in the front? Some famous architect from Seattle designed it."

"Can't believe they're going to take it down," I said.

"I don't know why everyone was so up in arms," Edith said. "Historical status for a Denny's? It's ridiculous. Change is change," she said again. "It happens. You need to learn to live with it."

Maybe so. But as we turned right up toward Market Street—the first time I'd been over there since before we started the project—I was kind of shocked at how different it was. Not the buildings themselves, but the businesses in them. I could almost see what all the fuss was about. We passed a fancy tea shop, a place that sold high-end stereo equipment, and some very nicely dressed folks wearing expensive sunglasses were drinking coffee outside the India

Bistro. Dads and kids with bicycles that had shock absorbers in the front were riding past Shakti Vinyasa Yoga across the street.

"It sure is different," I said. "I still like it, though. I've always liked how everything's so close together in Ballard."

"You can get from anywhere to anywhere in about five minutes," she said, and as if to prove it, she added, "Here we are."

It had, indeed, taken all of five minutes to get from Edith's out-of-the-way house to the hair salon in the middle of Market Street.

Everybody in the salon knew Edith, and she seemed to know everybody. She greeted each of them by name. If anyone seemed surprised to see Edith with an escort, they didn't say, and she didn't offer any explanation. She just asked them how long they thought she'd be there, and they told her about forty minutes. She asked me where I was going to go.

"Well, everything's about four minutes from here, Edith, so wherever I am, you all give me a call when you're five minutes from being done and I'll be here." I handed my card to the woman who ran the shop.

"Well, all right then," Edith said, and tilted her head to regard me with a clear, direct look. "Thank you, Barry."

It was a little early for lunch, but as long as I was on Market Street, I figured I'd continue down to the Totem House. That's one of the places that had been there a long time. It has a big, corny totem pole out front, and they sell a great seafood chowder. I picked up an order, and decided to drive down toward the beachfront.

A train was passing over the railroad trestle about a quarter-mile down the road. Just beyond that were the locks; by the flow of the water, it looked to me like they had just been opened. It's kind of amazing, when you think about it—down here, just west of downtown, is salt water. It's actually the other end of the canal from Edith's house, just five minutes away, and that's fresh water. The locks are what connects them. If they just opened the locks, I figured, a boat should be showing up here pretty quick. I like the locks—they have a viewing window down there, and when the salmon are running you can go in and watch them.

I drove past the marina, past the hundreds and hundreds of sailboats—that's one thing about Ballard that hasn't changed: They do love their boats. Just beyond the marina, there were a good hundred people sitting on benches and lying on blankets all over the beach. Nobody was in bathing suits, because it was still too cold, and besides, the water's about 54 degrees that early in the season, but a beach day is a beach day and everybody was out there with picnic lunches, only no bathing suits. Shirts and pants and beach balls. Kind of a funny scene.

It was just a few minutes after I got back to the trailer that my cell phone rang. Edith was ready to go home, so I jumped back in her car. She was waiting for me at the door of the salon; as I helped her back into the car, I got a big whiff of hairspray, one of those things that just transports you into another time, another era. I guess my mom must have used that kind of hairspray, or something, when I was a kid. It occurred to me that with everything else going on that morning, I hadn't really taken a moment to consider that here's this woman, well into her eighties, living a pretty solitary existence, and still going to the trouble of getting her hair done on a regular basis. It says something about her, and about her generation, I guess. For some reason I remembered those pictures you see of men at baseball games, years ago, in shirts and ties and fedoras. There was something a little more proper and formal about the way they went around in the world; it seemed like a measure of respect for each other, and for themselves, I guess, that's kinda been lost as time goes by.

When we got back to the house, I walked her to the front door. I still had never been inside the house, and I was kind of curious about how she lived in there, all alone all these years, but I wasn't going to find out this day.

She turned and smiled. "Thank you again, Barry. That was very neighborly of you."

"Not a problem. Let me know if you need anything else. Say, Edith?"

"Yes, Barry?"

"Your hair looks real nice."

Over the course of the next few weeks, I had more visits with Edith, always in the front yard. But one morning, she wasn't out where I expected to find her, so I knocked on her door, and she called from the kitchen for me to come in.

I will never forget that moment I stepped inside. Never. The first thing I saw was the end table. It was the table from my childhood. It was that classic fifties style—a plastic-laminate end table, dyed light tan to look like wood, small and rectangular, with a second shelf, half the size of the lower table, raised above it on two thin wooden side slats. On the higher shelf sat a lamp, and when I saw it I about fainted right then and there. Not only was the table the same, but this was the same exact lamp my family had when I was a kid as well. Same color and everything. It had a pink ceramic base shaped like an inverted vase, with little gold rods protruding from its top, and little gold metal balls on the ends of them. It was topped off with a wide translucent yellow paper shade, rimmed with a spiral metal edging and decorated with little brown palm fronds.

Looking at that table and lamp, this whooshing sensation came over me, like I was being transported back in time. And I was, really. For a second there, I was a kid again, walking into my mother's house, half expecting to get offered a peanut butter and jelly sandwich or get hollered at for not wiping my feet.

When I got my bearings back, I took a moment to look around. I couldn't believe how much stuff there was—all the books and records and CDs and figurines and photos—but still how very neat and tidy it all looked. Everything in its place.

The sun glinted off a metallic etching that was hanging on the wall. There were four of them, not quite gold, not quite silver; all street scenes from Venice. I wondered what the story was behind those.

When Edith came back into the room, I asked her about the etchings, but all she said was, "It's an interesting story. I'll have to tell you about it sometime." A very polite way, I guess, of saying "None of your business." So we moved on to other topics. She told me her friend Gail had stopped by earlier that day. Turns out Gail was just a kid growing up on the block when Edith first met her. In fact, Edith used to babysit for Gail and her sisters a lot. Gail had gone off to Alaska for a long time but came back a few years ago and now stopped by every now and then, and brought pictures of her and her sisters, all grown up now, and all of their children, all grown up as well.

It was nice to hear that her friend was still coming by after all these years, and, frankly, that Edith had some company besides me.

When I got back to the trailer I was surprised to see how late it had gotten. I'd wasted a good part of the morning with Edith, yakking about everything and nothing. I was finding it easier and easier to talk with her. Driving home that night, I thought about why that might be. What was it that was drawing me to her? You know how your kids spend an overnight at someone's house, and they come home, and the parents tell you how well-behaved and polite and helpful your kids were, and you think, "Are you talking about *my* kids?" There's something about kids, I guess, after a certain age, that they can relate to other people better than they can to their own parents. Maybe you're too close, or maybe it's their need to rebel, or something. Well, it never occurred to me that the same thing could still happen to you when you're all grown up. Somehow, I was already finding it easier to have conversations with Edith than I ever had with my own mom or dad.

I guess there were two reasons for that. For one thing, I felt like Edith didn't take things personally the way my own folks would. I guess that's just natural. Same with my own kids—no matter what they tell you, you can't help flashing back on things you've done and wondering if whatever problems they have are your fault in some way. But it was more than that. I also started realizing how much alike we were. Edith didn't sugarcoat things. She told you right out what she felt. I'm not so different. I see things pretty much in black and white. If something's not right, it's wrong. People can do what they should do, or they can not do it, but there usually isn't much question about what the right thing is. I felt really connected to Edith because, it seemed, she felt the same way. A little later, she would tell me stories of how she took in all these war orphans in England, and when I heard them I thought, What makes a person do something like that? But for her, it was simple: You do what has to be done.

I think I'm a lot like that. I hope I am, anyway. You do what needs to be done and you don't worry much about why or how you feel about it. You just do it. I think that's why it was so easy for us to talk. We shared something deep and true: an assumption about how you live your life.

Of course, it wasn't *always* easy to talk to Edith. One afternoon I saw these two guys coming down the street. They were quite a sight—both of them in their sixties, but still trying to be hip. Or some circa-1970 version of hip. One of them had a jacket and slacks and tie that looked like they came from three different secondhand stores. The other had gray hair and little round John Lennon glasses, like a refugee from a Woodstock reunion. To top it all off they were struggling along with a big hulking old video camera, and I guess they were going to interview Edith. Or thought they were, anyway. I figured it was about the same thing everybody always wanted to talk to her about—how she was standing up to the horrible developers and all that guff—but when I introduced myself to them and asked them what they were up to, I was surprised by the answer.

"Well, you know she used to be a spy," the guy with the glasses said, as matter-of-factly as if they said she used to be a telephone operator.

"Well, no, I didn't know that," I said. "Did she tell you that?"

"She sure did, man," he said. "And we have confirmed it through independent research."

Now, to be honest, these guys didn't seem to me like they had both oars in the water, so I didn't put much credence in what they were telling me. I left them to their business and went about mine. Later that afternoon, when I went over to chat with Edith in her front yard—I don't know if she'd ever talked to the guys or not, but they were gone now—I came right out and asked her about it.

And she came right out and told me to go to hell.

"Mind your own business!" she said. She was pulling some weeds and didn't even bother to look up. "Why the hell people dwell in the past is beyond me."

I thought, well, okay, I guess we won't go there today.

• • •

I was still thinking about Edith when I drove up to see my parents that weekend. I usually go up every couple of weeks. It's a pretty nice drive, once you get over the Tacoma Narrows Bridge, which is about halfway to their house. After that the roads get smooth and winding, following a serpentine route along the Hood Canal. You can see the canal and the Olympic Mountains behind them, and I don't think I've ever taken the drive without stopping to take a picture, of the fog rising up, or snow on the high peaks, or the clouds piling up and rolling over the mountains. Or the beaches, all covered with sun-bleached oyster shells. Every time it's a different view.

The traffic was light, so I pulled up to their place in a little over two hours. Their house is in the woods, on the thirteenth green of the Alderbrook golf course. Not a lot of manicured lawns up around there—there's too much rain. The biggest crop up here is moss.

I'm not sure if being with Edith made me want to see them more. When you spend time with someone who's a good fifteen years older than your parents, you start imagining them getting old, and I guess you start feeling guilty for not spending more time with them. Maybe it was that, or maybe it was the way my dad had been changing recently that made me feel like I really wanted to go see them more often. Mom and Dad both used to golf a lot, but lately Dad was going less and less. There were other changes as well: he had given up bridge altogether, for example. He'd make excuses about why he was quitting that stuff; they didn't ring true, but you didn't want to press him. I mean, if he doesn't want to talk about it then he doesn't want to talk about it—

but you'd still walk away feeling kind of puzzled and confused.

It probably wasn't the best day to spend together. My dad and mom were bickering all day—or to be honest, my dad was doing most of the bickering. I don't know why, but he was picking on my mom over the strangest little things, like the milk wasn't where it was supposed to be in the refrigerator. Or she'd left the clean laundry in the laundry basket instead of putting it away.

Late that afternoon we sat down in the family room, and I looked out the sliding windows at the thirteenth green. It was vacant right at the moment. Dad stretched back in his leather recliner and started telling me a story about the time he was eighteen and went on a NOAA ship to Alaska, to map the bottom of the ocean, at about the time a volcano was erupting there. Only, he couldn't think of the word *volcano*. Suddenly, he started acting angry at me: "Randy, what do you call that thing, for chrissakes?"

I don't know what freaked me out more: the fact that he was cursing (because he never cursed), the fact that he called me by my brother's name instead of my own, or the fact that he couldn't think of a simple word. It was scary, but I just let it go. "A volcano, Dad," I said. "Right. A volcano," he responded. "Well, you can imagine how excited I was. Eighteen years old and headed for Alaska! What an adventure."

As I listened to him spin the tale, my mother came in with a couple of cold glasses of water. As she bent over to put one on the little table next to Dad's chair, she paused, for just a second, and gave me a look, as though she was trying to tell me something. When I drove home that night, I remembered that look. I wondered what she was worrying about, and whether it was the same thing I was worrying about, too.

Lately, I'd been kind of impatient with my dad. I was just miffed at him. I couldn't put my finger on why exactly, but as I'd started the project in Ballard, I'd been getting more and more calls from my mom about him. Little things, mostly— the things couples argue about when they've been together, like my parents had, for more than fifty years—but it seemed like in the last few months there'd been more arguments than usual, and they'd gotten a little more serious. She noticed that he was flying off the handle more, over nothing, like I'd noticed when I'd been at their house. I'd tell him a story, and he'd mention it a little later, and my mom would correct him because he'd get the story mixed up, and out of nowhere he'd start yelling at her. It would just last a second, and normally you wouldn't think anything of it, but it was a little different from the way he usually was. My dad was the kind of guy who was always in control of everything.

I wouldn't show him that I was miffed, of course. I was raised to respect my elders, and that carried through to when I was an adult. I always did what he told me. I didn't always like it, but I didn't talk back. It's just the way we were raised. So even if I was getting pissed off now and again, I didn't say anything to him about it.

I don't think any of us is prepared for our parents to start to decline. I know I sure wasn't. It's denial, I guess. It's not that I didn't know what was happening to my dad. It was that I didn't want to know.

• • •

It was about six weeks after I took Edith to her first hair appointment that she asked me to take her again. I went over early that afternoon, and from the moment she entered the living room, I could tell that she was loaded for bear.

"I just want you to know I didn't appreciate that call this morning," she said, her voice full of venom. "You boys just keep hounding me to move, don't you? Well, I'm not moving, so you might as well stop bothering. Save your breath!"

I had no idea what she was talking about.

"Your friend over there at the company," she said. She was bundled up in a big brown sweater, and in her anger she seemed more hunched over than usual, like she was a snake all coiled up and ready to spring. "He tried to sound all polite. But I know what he's up to. I know what you're all up to. Forget it! I'm not moving. Why should I!"

Now, I'd been nothing but a perfect gentleman to Edith since I met her, but for the first time, I started to get angry. I know a lot of people saw Edith as a symbol of someone standing up for what's pure and true, or something like that. But that's not my battle, I thought. Don't make me the bad guy.

I'd been polite, and helped her out, and was taking her to her hair appointments and whatnot, and now I felt a little—betrayed, I guess.

"Listen up," I said. I was kind of surprised at how loud my voice was, but you know how it is: once you're on a roll, it's hard to stop. "None of this makes any difference to me. I work by the hour. If you stay or if you go, there's no benefit to me one way or the other. The job is the same number of hours either way. I build to the property line all the way around, no matter what that property line is. So don't put me in that."

I felt bad as soon as I let all that out. I mean, what am I doing, going off on some eighty-four-year-old woman? But Edith seemed almost relaxed by what I'd said. She moved forward, from the shadows in the corner, into the beam of light, flecked with dust, that streamed through the window. "All right then," she said. "Well, I apologize for that. I understand your position. I suppose we should get going now, shall we?" She seemed very calm. I guess she was trying to figure out just how far she could push me, and now that she knew where that line was, she could work from there. It was like we were both pushing right up to the property line. We just had to know what the boundaries were.

We went out to the car, and started up past the bridge. The sun was reflecting off the canal, and I put down the visor. A few fishermen passed in front of us at the stop sign near the Salmon Bay Café. That café's been there a long time but seemed a lot busier than I remembered it. There was a little traffic jam of people getting into the parking lot for lunch.

I felt like Edith and I had crossed a certain barrier that morning. By letting out our anger over the subject, we made it a little easier to talk about. So as I swung the car onto Market Street, I broached the subject again.

"Now, you know that I don't care one way or the other if you move, right?"

"Yes, I understand that," she said.

"Well, then, can I ask you a question?"

"Sure, sure," she responded.

"Why *don't* you want to move?"

She looked out the window.

"Why should I move?" she said, that crotchety tone creeping back into her voice. "Where on Earth would I go? I don't have any family. There isn't anywhere for me. This is my home."

"So it's not what people think, is it?"

She turned toward me. "It's never what people think."

I figured that was the end of it. But later that morning, after I brought her back from the hairdresser's, she opened up to me one more time.

I'd walked her back into the house just to make sure she'd gotten settled okay, reached down to turn on the lamp on the little side table, and was getting ready to go back to work. Edith was sitting on the couch and looked up at me. She seemed smaller, somehow; curled up quietly on the couch, not hunched or coiled like before.

"Barry, I want to tell you something," she said, her voice cracking a little bit.

I just turned, and was silent.

"My mother died right here, right on this couch," she said. The tears were starting to form again. "I came back to America to take care of my mother, and she always said she wanted to die at home, not in some—*facility*—and she made me promise, and I promised her. She died right here, Barry. And this is where I want to die. Right in my own home, on this couch. I'm not asking you to promise me, but I want you to know. Everybody wants me to move, and they all think it's best for me. But I know what I need. I need to be right here. This is my home. I want to live here and I want to die here. Do you understand?"

I looked down at this woman in the soft light filtering in through the thin curtains. She seemed so frail and so strong, at the same time. So vulnerable and so impenetrable. So needy, and yet so fiercely independent. I was moved by what she'd told me, and felt strangely protective of her. It was such a simple request, and it seemed so wrong that she should have to even fight for it. Even a Death Row prisoner gets to choose his last meal.

"I think I understand," I said. "Thanks for telling me that."

"Well, thank you for listening." She looked down, then back up at me. "Thank you for everything, Barry. You know what you are? You are a true human being."

I didn't know exactly what she meant by that, but I figured it was a good thing.

"Thanks, Edith. See you tomorrow."

"Yes. I'll see you tomorrow. Tell your wife I said hello. I'd love to meet her sometime."

And that was that. I felt, again, like we'd crossed some kind of border, into some new territory. It felt a little frightening and intriguing all at the same time, but more than that, it felt like we had become closer, part of each other's life in a way we hadn't been just a few minutes before.

I closed her door quietly and headed back to the construction trailer, trying to clear my mind, to focus on the tasks at hand. Feeling a little guilty for taking so much time off work that morning, but feeling pretty okay about it at the same time, for all that had occurred.

4

I was surprised by how self-sufficient Edith seemed in those first few months. She wasn't, however, getting by all on her own. A friend of hers, a fellow named Charlie, was coming by pretty regularly. Charlie looked like an unmade bed. Tall and wiry with long gray hair, he was younger than Edith but older than me, probably in his early sixties. He had that leftover-hippie kind of look. I'm not sure how they got to be friends, but they seemed to have that Old Ballard connection, and it went back a long ways. He did her shopping and helped around the house, although he didn't seem to stick around much once the chores were done. He said he was a project manager on construction sites, although when I tried to talk shop with him he'd change the subject. Still, he was helping Edith out, so I figured he was an okay guy.

Charlie's the one who first told me about the social workers, one morning in the late summer. "They're hovering again," he told me. Charlie had that way about him—he'd start up in the middle of a conversation, as though you'd already been talking and knew what he was talking about. It took a minute to catch up.

"Morning, Charlie. Who's hovering?" I asked him.

"Social workers. They're back at it again. If they think they're going to get her to move, they've got another think coming."

It took a while to get Charlie to tell the story in some kind of order I could understand, but once I got all the pieces of it, it made sense. The state had been after Edith for some time, concerned that she was not competent to take care of herself. They couldn't make her move—they couldn't prove that she was a danger to herself or anything—but they were apparently putting on a pretty strong push. Charlie said they kept coming around again and again, being persistent about how much better off she'd be, how much more comfortable she'd be, how much better her life would be, if only she'd let them bring her to a facility. I remembered how she used that word—*facility*—when she told me about her mother, how much disdain she had in her voice. It made me wince just hearing Charlie say it.

Now it made more sense to me why Edith was so touchy when guys from my office kept offering her more money to move. She must have felt she was battling on two fronts just to stay in her house—with the Bridge Group coming at her straight on and the social workers from the flank. I'm sure that, to Edith's ears, what they were both saying was, "You're not able to take care of yourself anymore. Let us do it for you."

I don't think anybody wants to hear that they can't take care of themselves. Certainly not a tough old bird like Edith.

Charlie took off, and I knocked on Edith's door. I wanted to ask her about the social workers, but when she called me to come in, I found her at a rickety little desk in the corner of the living room, typing at—well, I'm not sure what you call it anymore. It looked like a cross between a late-model electric typewriter and an early PC. The thing must have been twenty-five years old. It had a tiny square computer monitor and a dark gray keyboard with white keys—not like a modern keyboard, more like a typewriter—and she was pecking away at it, slowly. I saw the word *Whisperwriter* on it.

"Good morning, Barry," she said. "Excuse me for just a moment. My fingers don't work quite as well as they used to."

The sun was glinting off the monitor, so I couldn't quite make out what she was writing, but when she turned around she caught me looking at it, and I felt guilty for being so nosy.

"Just a little short story," she said, guessing at what I was trying to do. "The mind still works, but the goddamn fingers don't want to cooperate."

It was the first time I'd heard her curse.

"So, you're a writer?" I asked.

"Well, I've done my share," she said. "There's one of my books, right over there."

I looked at the counter where she was pointing, and there was a doorstop of a book, a big, bulky hardcover thing called *Where Yesterday Began*. The title was in red script, over the silhouettes of a man and woman looking at a sunset.

"Who's Dominelli?" I said, looking at the author's name.

"That's Dom-i-*li*-ni," she said, correcting me. "Domilini. That was the name I wrote under. I took it from . . ." But she didn't finish the sentence. Before I could ask, she was on her feet.

"Can't write anymore, dammit all," she said. "I'm getting a cup of tea. Can I offer you one?"

While she was shuffling off to the kitchen, I opened the book and looked at the inside cover. What I saw stopped me in my tracks.

ABOUT THE AUTHOR

E. Wilson Macefield (Domilini) was born in Oregon in 1921 and reared in Seattle and New Orleans. She served as an undercover agent during World War II. She was captured and interned at Dachau, from which she escaped, taking 13 interned Jewish children with her. She married a Yorkshire man, lived in England for thirty years, where she adopted and raised 27 children.

Following the death of her husband, she returned to the States to care for her mother. In 1984, she met and married an Old World Italian who was killed in an accident on their honeymoon. She has been writing for the greater part of her life, and has attained success in Europe.

"I cannot stop writing," she says, "whether it is read or not. It is imbedded in the soul." She wishes she might achieve the clarity of Maugham, and express the important truths of Locke, Lichens, and Poe.

This time, when she came back into the room, I was too intrigued to be embarrassed about my snooping. I didn't know where to start.

"Edith, it looks like you've lived quite a life," I said.

"I've lived quite a number of lives," she said.

"Who are all these children it talks about here? Where are they now?"

She began to tell me the wildest story. I can't even remember most of it now, it blew my mind so much. Apparently at some point she had come back to the States, but then was "summoned" back to England—that was her word—by a man she had met at a party. Apparently they had hit it off pretty well. He was a very rich man, and he had asked her if she had unlimited funds what she would do with the money.

"I told him there's only one thing a moral person can do in this moment in time," she said, her good eye focused not on me but on a spot somewhere out the window, as though she was trying to see something far away. "Create an orphanage for all the children left without parents by the awful war." So he brought her back to England, and gave her a castle in Cornwall to start the orphanage.

"Gave her a castle in Cornwall." There's a sentence I bet no one I know has ever heard in their lives.

She went on, telling me how she went to Scotland and bought some sheep to raise at the castle.

Suddenly, Edith fell silent. I tried to ask her more. I mean, I had a million questions. Led an escape from Dachau?

Married a Yorkshire man? Was he the guy with the castle? Was he Domilini, or was that the "Old World Italian"?

But I wasn't getting any answers. She was done, for now. "The past is the past," she said, and that pretty much ended it. "This tea isn't hot enough. I'm going to go warm it up. Lukewarm tea tastes too much like piss, if you ask me."

She tottered off back to the kitchen, her teacup rattling on its saucer. She crossed the bright ray of sunlight streaming in through the windowpane, dust motes swirling in the light, all my questions just hanging in the air with them.

The questions I had about my dad got answered that summer. He was still slipping, no doubt about it. He'd forget my sister Malinda's name, which drove her kind of bats. Or he'd ask my mother a question, and five minutes later ask the same thing again. He was having trouble doing math in his head—something he'd always been pretty good at—and that would make him really angry. Angrier than it ought to, frankly. He'd start trying to figure something out, like what's 15 percent of $150, and the next thing you know he'd be cursing a blue streak. As I said, it was strange to hear my dad curse, and that as much as anything made us wonder if something was up. He wouldn't talk about it, though. He's from that generation where you just buck up and hold whatever's bothering you inside, so we mostly just let it go.

Except for Malinda. Malinda's my older sister, and the pushiest of us three kids. I mean that in a nice way. She's the one who's going to say enough's enough, let's get done what needs to get done, period. And that's what she did in this situation. It was at her urging—her insistence is more like it—that my mom took my dad for tests. They did all kinds of tests those first couple of weeks—dexterity tests, memory tests, blood tests, brain scans, you name it. My dad was none too pleased about it all, but he went along with it.

And it's a good thing he did, because when the diagnosis came back, it was what everybody was afraid of but nobody had said.

Alzheimer's.

It's a hell of a blow, when you hear your dad has Alzheimer's. It doesn't matter how old you are; your dad is still a huge figure in your life, especially a dad like mine, who was always competent, in charge, and in control. You can't picture him becoming disabled, forgetful, unable to care for himself. I tried not to imagine the road ahead of him too much. It was just too hard to think about.

But oddly enough, for my dad, it was just the opposite. I went up to see him right after the diagnosis came through, and I could see right away that he was a lot calmer. It was almost like his frustration wasn't about forgetting things; it was about not knowing why he was having the problem. Being given an answer, a name for the problem, seemed to make him feel better. He was always a problem-solver; give him a situation and he'd figure out what to do. Now that he knew what the problem was, it was almost like he was saying, Oh, well, why didn't you say so? Now we know what we're dealing with so we can figure out how to deal with it.

We knew it wouldn't always be that easy, of course. But

at least some of the steam had gone out of the pressure cooker.

As I drove home that evening, I found myself thinking about going fishing with my dad when I was a kid. There was one time up in Canada, the first time he taught me how to start a fire. We'd gotten rained off the lake, and climbed up on a hill, on a game trail under the trees. There were a bunch of us there, huddled together: my dad, my brother, some friends of the family—all guys, that morning. The women were more fair-weather fishing types, and had stayed back at the campground. I watched carefully as my father gathered up some pine needles, put a pine cone right in the middle of them, and leaned some dried sticks from dead branches on the pine cone. He lit the pine needles with a match. While the fire was starting up, he found a piece of willow, or maybe it was maple, and cleared the bark off it. He gutted the trout we'd pulled out of the lake before the rain started, and stuck the stick through the back of the fish, and out its mouth, and held it over the fire. Maybe it was just the moment, but that trout tasted about ten times better than it ever could have tasted at home. I can still taste the crisp skin, the buttery flesh, the feel of the oils from the meat of the fish sliding on the sides of my tongue.

It was usually a family affair when we went camping, and sometimes another family went with us. But as I continued my drive home that night, my thoughts drifted to the time I got to go fishing with my dad, just the two of us. I was probably about twelve. My mom had taken my brother and sister to visit some relatives in North Carolina, but I couldn't go, because I had a paper route. So that weekend, my dad took me fishing over to Nason Creek, near the Wenatchee National Forest. To get there you drove over Stevens Pass, which was really cool, especially for a twelve-year-old. Up there in the mountains, you felt like you could see a thousand feet down to the bottom, to where there were boulders, vine maples, and the beginnings of a river. On the opposite side, near the bottom, there's an old highway and a train rail. The rails had a shed roof over them to try to keep the snow off, and whatever else an avalanche would bring down. It was abandoned a long time ago because it was too hard to maintain, so now it just sat there, and as we drove by it looked like an old toy train set that someone had just gotten too old to play with.

It was really special, having my dad all to myself. He was a soft-spoken guy, but a jocular one, and as we came down off the mountain and glided along those long, curvy, tree-lined stretches of Route 2, the sky big and high around you, the clouds puffy and still, he was doing what he always loved to do, which was give you little brain teasers, stuff to make you think. Like coming up with oxymorons. "I got one," he said. "Jumbo shrimp." I don't know why, but at the time that struck me as about the funniest thing I'd ever heard.

We slept that night in a camper on the back of his pickup truck, and as I was falling asleep, my dad started telling me fishing stories. I'd caught more fish than he had that first day, and he said, well, he was just waiting. "I don't like to mess with the little ones, the way you do," he said, just a hint of that jocular tone in his voice, like you couldn't tell how serious he was. "I'm waiting for the big one. You'll see." We went out early the next morning, and sure enough, about an hour before it was time for us to head back, his line went tight, and he landed the biggest salmon I had ever seen. He needled me about it the whole ride home: "Don't you worry, Barry, those little fish you caught will taste pretty nice too," or "Well, I guess it's good that you didn't try to land any big fish this trip; wouldn't want you to hurt yourself." I pretended to be ticked off when he razzed me, but he could tell by the look on my face that I was about as high as the clouds. I gave him a playful punch on those big strong arms of his, as he steered the pickup back into the setting sun, headed home, just my dad and me and a big old cooler full of fish.

5

Edith's house, which looked a little sad and lonely to begin with, was looking even sadder once all the buildings around it were torn down. It resembled some last outpost of a bombed-out village after World War II, which probably wasn't all that unfamiliar to Edith, given what I was learning about her past. The block was empty now except for Edith's house, and a place called Mike's Chili Parlor on the far back corner of the lot. Mike serves some decent chili dogs—they got kind of famous, actually, when he appeared on the TV show *Drive-Ins, Diners, and Dives*—and I will say I ate a lot of them during the project. The Bridge Group decided early on not to try to obtain that building, because they were afraid somebody would go after historic status for Mike's. He's been there since about a week before forever. Besides, he was outside the perimeter of the shopping mall site anyway, so it wasn't a big deal. Not like Edith's house.

There were other issues on the project, though. For one

thing, the soil on the site was contaminated with lead. It wasn't that much of a surprise; lead is usually a by-product of manufacturing. The material was all fill that had been brought in back in the twenties to bring the site above sea level. The fill must have been contaminated with the residual lead from some kind of plant—a smelter, maybe—and there was a little arsenic in the soil, too. It all had to go.

So there we were, digging twelve feet down on a rectangular city block, which meant we had 48,000 tons of contaminated material to dig out and haul away so it could be disposed of properly. It was a long and noisy process, but Edith didn't seem to mind. In fact, I think she was enjoying all the hubbub going on all around her. She would come out and watch the goings-on and wave to the workers when they'd walk by, and they'd wave back with a friendly "Hi, Edith, how's it going?" All in all, a pretty copacetic relationship.

It wasn't just the soil we were concerned about. On a job like this, when you're digging a huge hole, you also have to worry about the pressure of trucks going by on the adjacent roads. You have to sink massive I-beams, three feet wide, into the ground for support. You have to stick them twice as far in as they're going to stick out, so basically the beams were about forty feet long. It was a big deal, but it had to be done: no beams, and the road could have collapsed into the hole.

You never know what you're going to find once you start digging. One afternoon, when I was walking by the far end of the lot, I noticed that the track hoe had something big in its jaw. As I got closer, I saw a big metal tank of some kind, maybe an old oil drum or something. My first thought was, hey, we could cut that in half and make a nice little site barbecue—but when I got a little closer, I could see that it was actually shaped like something more dangerous.

A bomb, in fact.

It looked like one of those bombs they used for carpet-bombing during World War II. It didn't have fins on the back, but it did have four bolts where the fins could be attached. I asked the track hoe operator what he thought it was, and he said, "I dunno, but there's a whole bunch of them right over there."

Sure enough, there was a pile of about ten of those things, sitting in plain view. I immediately told the track hoe operator what I thought they were. He got white as a sheet, and just froze in place.

I told everyone to move away from the site, and dialed 911.

"What is your emergency, sir?" the operator asked.

"I think I've found a bomb," I said. I mean, how else was I going to put it?

There was silence on the other end. Finally, she spoke, as though she was speaking to a crazy person: "A what, sir?"

I figured she might think she's talking to a crazy person, but she's not going to be talking to a dead crazy person. I told her again that I thought I'd found a bomb.

Within minutes, two police cars showed up. They were treating the whole incident pretty nonchalantly until they saw the thing, at which point their demeanor became all business. They called the bomb squad from their cell phones, because they didn't want to put it out over the radio and give the media a chance to get wind of it and panic everybody. I noticed that one of the workers on the site—one of the environmental guys who worked for the owner—was still at his post. "Excuse me," I said to him. "What part of 'this could be a bomb and it could blow up' did you not understand?" He got up and, with a big sigh, slowly walked away.

Ten minutes later, the bomb squad, the FBI, and a bunch more police cars were on the scene, along with my bosses from Ledcor. We watched from the street as officers swarmed all over the site. I went up to the guy at the big black bomb squad truck parked on the street, and asked him if he'd like me to open a gate so he could pull the truck onto the site. "No, I got a million bucks' worth of equipment on here," he said. "Anything blows up, I can't take a chance."

I looked over at all the cops.

"Well, there sure are a lot of guys standing around the thing," I said. "Are they okay to be there?"

"We lose those officers," he deadpanned, "we can get new ones. But this equipment is hard to replace."

Just then, the guy who had been so reluctant to take this seriously was striding up to me. He seemed to think it was his job to read me the riot act: he was "officially putting me on notice" that Ledcor was responsible for this site. He started grilling me about why we weren't securing the perimeter, and telling me that the safety of everyone was our responsibility. He was just ranting. I tried to calm him down a few times, and point out that the police had the scene under control, but the more I tried to reassure him, the wilder his ranting got. Finally, I put one hand on his collar, grabbed his arm with the other, and escorted him off the premises. The cops looked over and didn't bat an eye, except for one who I swear was trying to stifle a big grin.

After an hour or so, the bomb squad X-rayed the whatever-it-was. After that, and after the yellow Labrador bomb-sniffing dogs had gone over the scene, the bomb squad declared that whatever the thing was, it wasn't a bomb. They had my guy break it open with a track hoe, which was a tense moment, but there was no ordnance inside. (We never did find out what the thing was; they brought in all sorts of experts but no one could come up with an answer. The best guess was that it was an old "dolphin"—fishing boats use them for stabilizers. You put them out on the end of a long stick, one on each side of the boat, a little like the way a tightrope walker uses a long pole to steady himself.)

Like I said, when you start digging, you never know what you're going to find.

We finished digging the hole sometime around November, which was the perfect time to start digging something else: clams. Every year Evie and I take the kids up to Ocean Shores in the fall, and again usually in the spring, and this year was going to be no different. We drove up on a Friday night, and a couple of friends and their kids caravanned with us. We always go with friends, and usually take someone who's never done it before, to pass it along, because it's an experience they'll never forget.

We always stay in a condo at the Polynesian, a nice place right there on the beach, and after we got unpacked we sat around drinking and yakking while all the kids played at the pool. But we didn't make too late a night of it, because we were getting up really early. You do your clamming at what they call the "minus tide." There are four tides every day, two highs and two lows, but a few times a year you get the minus tide, which can be two feet lower than the regular low tide, perfect for digging clams. This weekend, the lowest tide happened to be in the morning, so that's when we went.

We trucked out there about 8 a.m., lugging our shovels and clam guns, me and Willy in our chest waders, Evie and Kelsey in their hip boots. When you get to the beach, it's a pretty wild sight: five thousand people, maybe more, strewn along three miles of beach. I was a little sorry we weren't going at night, because that's really an astonishing sight: all those people carrying Coleman lanterns or miner's headlamps, thousands of lights as far as the eye can see. Like some gigantic, living Chinese lantern you're all building together.

It was a cold, nasty, wet morning, but we were all in pretty good spirits (especially the adults. A good Bloody Mary can really set the tone for a good day. Breakfast of Champions, we always call it).

A bunch of us were toting the clam guns. A clam gun is a three-foot-long metal tube, like a car cylinder, with a T-shaped handle at the top, so you can grab the ends of the T and shove the cylinder into the sand. There's a hole at the top of the handle about the size of a pencil eraser. You hold your thumb over the hole after you shove the cylinder down into the sand, so it creates a vacuum when you pull it back out, and the clam gun yanks a big clump of sand up with it.

We all gathered pretty close together, and started looking

for clam shows. If you stomp on the ground, the razor clam will leave a little "show"—it will pull its neck down and leave a small dimple in the sand, like a golf ball hit there. That's where you hit the sand with your clam gun. The clam is usually in the clump you pull out, or sitting right there in the hole. You've got to be fast, though. Razor clams are big, the size of your open palm, and they dig pretty fast.

Kelsey was already down on the ground, her face pressed into the sand, her arm way down in a hole. In a couple of seconds she came up with her first clam. Willy was the best at it though: the legal limit was fifteen clams, and after maybe a half-hour he'd already hit his limit, so there was nothing left for him to do but taunt the rest of us. "Better get moving, Dad, or I'll start digging your limit! Mom's, too!" By this point we're all ridiculously sandy and wet and muddy, there's grit in every pore of your body, but we're all laughing, because I guess when you're that miserable and cold and wet there's nothing else to do. But there's also just a great feeling of being out on an adventure with your family and friends, not to mention carrying on a family tradition. My dad used to take me clamming, but those were littlenecks, which are very different. They live at the rocky beaches, and they don't dig very far down, so you kinda just rake them up. With razor clams, it's a battle.

A battle you usually win, of course, although you sometimes have a couple of casualties. The rule is never turn your back to the ocean, but this morning Kelsey forgot just for a minute, and a rogue wave came and knocked her on her butt. She stood up sputtering and soaking wet, and you couldn't tell if she was going to laugh or scream. She did both, of course, which was about the funniest thing that could happen at eight in the morning on a freezing beach in Washington, the sky lightening to the color of the fender on an old Ford, your daughter shaking her head like a wet German shepherd, and your muddy wife collapsing against you because she's laughing too hard to stand up.

When we all hit our limit, we went to the cleaning station with our clams. The way it works is, you plunge the clams in boiling water just for a few seconds to open them up, then drop them in cold water to stop them from cooking. It's a whole process: once they're open you pull the clam out of the shell, and pinch the belly and the digger off—the digger is what you call their little foot—then cut the digger off the belly with a pair of scissors. The digger's pretty thick, so you fillet that in half. You have to slice the neck open too, where it sticks out of the body of the clam, to get all the sand out.

It's a lot of work, but it's worth it. Later, we went over to my friends Joe and Kelly's unit, for a big old clam fry: You flour them, then dip them in an egg wash, roll them in some cracker crumbs, and fry them up in butter and olive oil. Now, when you've been as wet and cold and muddy as you get out there on the beach, you could probably fry up an old boot and it would taste delicious, for all the effort you went through; so when you get razor clams fried up like this, all I can say is, if it ever gets any better than that, I don't know when. I really appreciated that moment, and I'm glad I did, because I had no idea that it would be the last clam-digging trip we'd take for quite a while.

• • •

November's a pretty dank and dreary time in Seattle, and I hadn't seen Edith in about a week, so the day I got back I figured I'd go check on her and let her know that things would get a little quieter now that we were done moving earth and setting the I-beams. I knocked on her door, but there was no answer.

It was Charlie who filled me in, when I spotted him the next day.

"She's still at the hospital," he said. "Probably be a little while before they move her on to rehab"—picking up in the middle of the conversation, as always, and leaving out what the hell had happened.

What the hell had happened, he finally told me, was that she'd fallen down the stairs and broken three ribs.

I felt guilty as hell. I hadn't been working next to Edith's house for the last few weeks, so I hadn't been paying much attention to her. I know there's nothing I could have done to stop her from falling, but guilt is guilt; it doesn't always need a reason.

I told Charlie that I was worried about her in the hospital. "You know, with old people, they lie around the hospital, next thing you know, they get pneumonia, and . . ." I couldn't bring myself to finish the thought. But Charlie knew what I was about to say, and his response kind of startled me.

"Well, I've been expecting her to die for ten years, and she hasn't done it yet," he said. I thought maybe I detected a note of annoyance in his voice, but I didn't know what to make of it, so I just let it go.

I didn't see Edith for the next few weeks. I wanted to go visit her at the hospital, but I wasn't sure that was my place. I didn't want to overstep my boundaries, I guess. It's one thing to wander over for a chat when your trailer is forty feet away from someone's door; another to show up when they're in a hospital bed downtown. It just didn't feel right to me. I kept wondering if it was okay for me to go visit, or if I'd be intruding. That and, to be honest, work was getting really busy, and a lot of days just got away from me.

Later, when I heard about who did visit her, and what happened, I'm kind of glad I wasn't there.

I was at a site meeting, the kind of meeting we have once a week to make sure everyone's on the same page, when Angela, one of the architects on the project, told me what had gone down.

Apparently Rick and some of the other fellows on the project got ahold of Charlie, and they all went to see Edith, and brought her a contract. They had upped their offer.

To one million dollars.

I couldn't believe it.

But knowing Edith, I had no trouble believing what happened next.

Apparently, Edith had gotten really enraged at them all— she was insulted that they'd come around while she was still recuperating. Bunch of vultures, she called them. She kicked them out, and told them exactly where they could put their one million dollars. She was even more pissed that they had brought Charlie, because she was a full-grown woman and able to make her own decisions.

"Well, that didn't go so well, did it," I said to Angela.

"No, it went kinda sideways," she said.

A few weeks later, I was headed to the construction trailer, and there was Edith, out in front of her house, feeding the birds. I stopped to say hello, and we chatted a bit. She seemed even more frail than she had before, but I didn't say anything about that.

"So, has Charlie been by to stock you up on groceries?" I asked.

"No," she said, "I don't think he's going to be around for a bit."

She was trying to be matter-of-fact about it, but there was clearly a lot more to this than she was saying. I had to prod her a little, but finally she told me that when she turned down the million-dollar offer from the owners, Charlie got furious. Really furious. He had the keys to her house and threw them at her, and said, "You're on your own!" and stormed off.

I was taken aback by that. I couldn't figure out why he would be so angry. It's her house; it's her decision. I asked Edith if I could help her out in any way. "Thank you, that's very kind," she said, "but this nice woman I met at the rehab center came by. Joanie, her name is. She and her husband volunteer down there. They've been helping me out. She's inside right now."

I was glad to hear it. Over the course of the next few weeks I also saw Edith's friend Gail once or twice; she was coming to visit Edith a little more often these days, and we'd stop and chat a bit. She was on Edith's side—she didn't see any reason Edith should move if she didn't want to. And Joanie was around pretty frequently, coming in and out of Edith's, bringing bags of groceries, tending to the lawn, and such. But then suddenly she disappeared and Charlie showed back up. When I asked Edith what was going on, why Joanie wasn't around anymore, she said, in that blunt way of hers, "I just told her to get the hell out of here."

Once again it took me a while to piece it all together, but between Edith and Charlie I got the facts. Edith had fallen again. She wasn't injured this time, but she couldn't get up, and had an accident on the floor. A bowel movement, to be blunt. Joanie was horrified. She cleaned it up, but immediately called the social workers. Edith wasn't the slightest bit happy about that, because they all started talking again about having Edith declared incompetent. Edith didn't know who to turn to, so she called Charlie. He came over to help her out—and to tell her he was moving, to Arlington, more than an hour's drive away. He said he'd still bring her groceries on Tuesdays, but you could tell that things had started spinning out of control for Edith. For the first time, she seemed a little out of control herself.

I can trace everything that has happened since back to that moment. It wasn't like I made some big decision to step in or anything like that. It didn't even seem like a big deal at the time. But it was at that moment that the lives of Barry Martin and Edith Wilson Macefield started to converge, in a way no one could have anticipated. Especially me.

• • •

When things change the way they did, it's like the game you play of trying to watch the moon move across the sky when you're out fishing before dawn. You think you see a little movement, but it's really just an illusion caused by a passing cloud. Then after a while your mind wanders, and when you look back at the moon, which used to be right over here, it's suddenly way over there.

Now that Joanie was gone, and Charlie was only coming around once a week, and with those broken ribs still making it hard for her to get around, Edith needed a little more help. A few days later she called me to get her hair done again. Then she called me again to tell me she had a doctor's appointment, and that she really didn't feel like driving, could I take her? And I said, well, of course, and so then I began taking her to all her doctor appointments. Then, the next thing I knew, I was scheduling the appointments myself. It was easier that way because I could set them up around my work.

One afternoon she was wondering aloud about what she was going to fix herself for lunch. I told her one of the boys was going to McDonald's and that we'd be happy to bring her something. I suggested a Big 'N Tasty, and when I described it, she said, "Oh, yes, that sounds good, with lettuce and tomato." It was the first time in my life I'd ever heard anyone actually pronounce it "to-MAH-toe" without trying to be funny. "Don't bring me any of those fries, though," she said. "They're too fattening."

I sent one of the boys out for the food, and told him to bring back a vanilla shake, as well. That was the day I learned what a sweet tooth Edith had. I mean, she'd stick her straw in that vanilla shake and would not take her mouth off it until that shake was gone. After that she'd start calling me about once a week and say, "Can I have a hamburger and one of those vanilla things?"

As time went by I started bringing lunch more often and going to more of her appointments. Before I knew it, weeks turned into months, and we were spending a lot of time together. As I said, it didn't seem very strange to me, because when you make a change so gradually, it's hard to notice any one point where it feels like you've turned a corner, until you look back and realize that you have.

Usually when I'd spend time at Edith's we'd just talk about nothing—the weather and the neighborhood and such. I hadn't really asked her about all the brouhaha that was building up around her in the papers—all the stuff about how she'd become a hero in a lot of people's eyes, and such. Or if I did mention it, she'd always brush it off and change the subject.

But this one day, I guess she felt like opening up.

"Edith," I said, "how are you doing with all this? Is the noise bothering you? Are we starting too early or working too late? Do you take a nap in the afternoons?"

"Oh, you're fine, Barry," she said, struggling to take a bite of her Big 'N Tasty. I noticed that her hands were shaking more than they had before. "It used to be that the city transfer was back here, you know. At five in the morning, the garbage trucks would be rolling in and out. I knew the gentlemen who were working over there. Nice young men, like your-self. I know everyone has a job to do. I can't let that affect me. I worked hard when I was a young woman, and I know what it is to put in an honest day's work. You can't ever fault any-one for that."

It was the second time she'd mentioned working. She had said something about working for the British government, and there was that blurb in the book about her working as an undercover agent. And then, of course, there were those two guys who'd told me she used to be a spy. I was really curious. "What exactly did you do, Edith?"

She turned her head and gave me a strange half-smile. Then she paused, like she was weighing how much to tell me. I felt like I was watching someone standing on the edge of a pool, deciding whether to jump in or just dip a toe to see how the water feels.

"My good friend, I have done many, many things," she said. "In the span of twenty years, I lived three different lives. You do know I was a spy for the British in Nazi Germany."

Now, that's not a sentence you usually hear over a Big 'N Tasty.

I tried not to sound too stunned. So what those two goofy guys had said, what it said in the book blurb, was true! Edith didn't seem to remember that the first time I asked her about it she'd told me to go to hell. "Go on," I said.

"Well, yes, I worked for the British government. I was just a teenager at the time. I went to the American government to get a job. This was in the early part of the war, before the United States was really involved. They wouldn't put me to work because they said I was too young. I was fourteen at the time, but I really wanted to work, and I wanted to do something important, do you understand? Well, I had an uncle who knew people in England, and he said he could get me a job working for the British government. So he flew me over there. I loved England. I really loved it. The people are so . . ."

She started to trail off. I saw her struggling with her sandwich again, and half-rose from my chair to help her, but then thought better of it. I decided to just wait and let her start up again when she wanted to.

"I was a music student, you know," she said, starting on a different tack. "I was quite good on the clarinet. My cousin Benny gave me my first one. You do know Benny Goodman is my cousin."

It crossed my mind, not for the first time, that maybe this lady was just a bit loony tunes after all. But I didn't say anything.

"In any case I knew a great deal about music. And that was my 'in.' There was a man at the consulate there who took a good deal of interest in me. I wasn't sure why the British would be so interested in a teenaged clarinet player, but then of course one day they took me into a room with a number of gentlemen, all in dark suits, and told me that they thought my age and musical ability would form the perfect cover for a spy. In Germany."

"A spy in Germany," I repeated, trying to get the words to sound like they made sense. "What was that all about? I mean, what did you do?"

At that, Edith became very quiet. She dabbed at her lips

with the napkin, then put it down carefully on the table and placed what remained of her sandwich on top of it. She turned toward the window, then took a deep breath and let out a big sigh, like she was blowing the memories away.

"Are you taking me to the doctor's tomorrow?" she asked.

"Of course I am, Edith," I said. "Two o'clock. They called in your prescription already. I'll go pick it up this afternoon on my way downtown." I could see that she didn't want to talk about the past anymore, so I let it drop. I think I was coming to understand how it worked with Edith. She'd open a door for a while, but then for whatever reason she'd decide it was time to close it. It didn't make any sense for me to try to jam a foot in there and keep it open. I had to take it as it came.

Shortly after that, we passed another kind of milepost. Charlie called Edith up one morning and said, "The weather's too bad, I'm not going to make it over there this week to get your groceries." So Edith called me up, crying and having a fit that Charlie wasn't coming and she was going to starve to death.

I'm surprised that in all her stories she never told me she was an actress, because she really seemed to have a flair for the dramatic. I went over and showed her that she still had food left. She seemed to favor Stouffer's frozen TV dinners, or at least that's what Charlie seemed to think she favored— but I offered to run to the store for her anyway. I figured I could spare the ten minutes, and it sure seemed to make a big difference to her.

I think it was about two weeks later that I went over after work and was sitting and talking to her when I heard the buzzer go off. "Oh, that's my dinner," she said, and I offered to get it for her.

So I got up and went into the kitchen and put my hand on top of the stove to open the oven door, and just about burned my hand off. It was one of those old 1950s ovens with no insulation, and it's as hot on the outside as it is on the inside, and I'm thinking, here's Edith with skin about as thin as tissue paper and about as sure on her feet as a one-legged penguin, and I just know one of these days she's going to stumble and fall and burn herself bad on that oven.

So that's how I started cooking her dinner every night.

It was no big deal. I had it down to a science. I could put a TV dinner in, go to the grocery store, buy her groceries, turn around and come back, put the groceries away, and dinner would be ready. Other nights I'd go back to the trailer and get a few last bits of paperwork done, or just sit and talk to Edith.

Edith had this belief that you had to preheat the oven for thirty minutes or things wouldn't cook properly; she made me set a timer on the oven, and if I put the food in before the timer went off, she'd raise holy hell. Sometimes, if I didn't have the thirty minutes to wait, I'd just hit the button so the buzzer would buzz, and she'd believe that I'd preheated the oven, and we could go on from there. These are the small things that can either drive you crazy, when you're taking care of an old person, or you can just accept and move on. I decided to go the accept-it-and-move-on route.

I did talk to her about getting a microwave, but she wouldn't hear of it. "House isn't designed for a microwave," she'd say. "House is a hundred years old and the wiring wasn't set up for running that newfangled stuff." Or "Things don't stay hot when you microwave 'em. They don't get hot in the middle."

So, instead of trying to change her mind, which I never could anyway, I just kept making her dinner. It was easy, and it was kind of comforting. For both of us, to tell you the truth. Because on the nights when we'd just sit and talk and wait for her TV dinner to cook, she started telling me more stories. And she sure had some doozies.

Case in point: One evening I noticed a picture sitting on the dusty bookcase in the living-room part of the first floor. It was Edith, wearing wire-rimmed glasses and holding a clarinet and looking for all the world like Benny Goodman.

"Edith, how old were you when you started playing the clarinet?" I said.

"Well, I never was much good at it. My cousin Benny gave me one of his old clarinets, that's how it started."

It was the second time she'd mentioned that, and I was really wondering if it was true or not. It got me thinking, so I started flipping through her Benny Goodman albums—she had a bunch of them—and what I saw on one of them really startled me.

It was autographed, and it said, "To my Cousin Edith. With Love, Benny."

Well, la-di-da-di-da. What do you know.

"Um, Edith, when was the last time you saw your cousin Benny?" I asked her.

"Well, that would be a long time ago. He died about twenty years ago, you know, but it was a long time before that. It was back in the Chicago days."

I figured I'd bite at that little bit of bait. "Who else was around in the Chicago days, Edith?"

"Oh, you know, that whole gang. Tommy Dorsey, Jimmy Dorsey, that whole Lombardo gang, Guy and Victor and Carmen. Guy was the bandleader but I think the brothers were the ones with the talent. We traveled around a lot, so you'd catch them in various places. Maurice Chevalier would show up from Paris now and then. Guy we'd mostly see in New York. That was the thing, you know, to be with Guy Lombardo on New Year's Eve. Tommy Dorsey was the nicest man. I remember when he was just coming up, he needed some money, so I bought one of his old saxophones from him. I don't know why—I mean, what was I going to do with a saxophone?—but I thought I should help him out."

Edith was fussing with something on her sweater, like the fact that a button was coming loose or whatever was as important as the fact that she once bought a saxophone from Tommy Dorsey. I tried to pepper her with questions, but as usual, she dropped the subject as quickly as it came up.

I looked down at the record album. "To my Cousin Edith. With Love, Benny."

The buzzer on the oven went off. It was like the oven was saying, "Time's up."

6

The owners of the project kept talking to me about Edith. They never came out and asked me to set up a meeting, but they couldn't understand why she was hanging on to that place. I really don't think they were trying to take advantage of her. They saw her with this house, isolated on a lonely block, a house that had seen better days, with dinky old stairs that couldn't possibly be good for an old woman, and a kitchen that belonged in the Smithsonian, and they thought, if she had some money she could get a nice rambler, and hire someone to help her out, and life would be better. They knew they'd blown it when they met with her at the hospital—that was pretty clear—but they were, cautiously and pretty politely, looking for another chance.

So one day I told Edith about Rick Gervais, one of the owners, who used to be a defensive back for the San Francisco 49ers. I told her Rick was a really good guy—which he is— and I asked if she'd be willing to sit down with him, and about a week later we all got together. It was funny to see that big defensive back squeezing into a chair in that tiny house, I have to say, like a storybook giant had come down the beanstalk to visit the little people. The meeting was cordial—Edith even offered everyone tea and Walkers Shortbread cookies—and Rick told her how easy they would make it for her if she moved. He said he'd bring someone into her house to take pictures, and set up the new house to look exactly the same. He mentioned the million dollars again, as casual as could be, like someone offers you a million dollars for your tiny little house every day of the week. He didn't stop there, either: On top of the million bucks, he said, they would buy a new house for her, and she could live in it for the rest of her life, and it would revert back to them after that. Edith didn't blink.

"I'm not sure why I need a million dollars," she said. "If I get sick it probably won't cover the medical bills, and if I don't get sick I don't need it. And if you're going to make the new place look just like this one, well, this place already looks just like this one, so why should I bother?"

That was just about the end of that. As Rick was leaving, though, Edith allowed as how she'd think about it, and I think she was actually starting to mull it over. I still couldn't decide if we were doing what we thought was best for Edith, or what we wanted to be best for Edith because it was best for us. I didn't know how often that question would come up over the course of the next year.

After Rick left, Edith started fussing with some of the little figurines on the windowsill, like they'd moved themselves around in the night. She was silent, and I wasn't quite sure what she was thinking.

The amount of time I was spending with Edith started creeping up on me. Between making dinner and bringing her lunch, and taking her to her hair appointments and doctor appointments and all, it was getting to be a pretty consuming thing. Fortunately for me, Evie and the kids were about as supportive as you could ever ask your family to be. Evie was pretty amazing about it all. She never outright said she was proud of me for what I was doing, but I could tell from her manner and the questions she'd ask that she believed I was doing the right thing. She's the kind of woman who appreciates people who do the right thing. Like Gail, who still took the time to pay a call on the woman who babysat her as a child. You have to respect someone like that.

To tell the truth, it wasn't affecting our lives all that much. Most of the time when I got off work, I knew I could do Edith's grocery shopping, or stop by and cook her dinner, and still get home about as fast as if I'd spent the time sitting in rush-hour traffic. And it's not like all of a sudden you can decide, well, I'm not going to do this anymore. Not if I wanted to sleep at night, anyway.

And in the back of my mind there was that thing she told me. That there was a way she wanted to live the rest of her life, and a way she wanted to die. I kept thinking, well, there's no reason in the world that she shouldn't. And if she needs a little help getting there, then so be it.

A few days later I was having lunch with Edith again, and she was talking about how all the reporters kept calling her up and bugging her for interviews. I told her that that would drive me crazy.

"I don't mind it," she said. "I just tell them to leave me the hell alone. Then I don't think about it anymore."

"Well," I said, "you're a better man than I am, Gunga Din."

At that, she gave me that funny faraway look and put down her sandwich. She stood up and began to recite:

> "In India's sunny clime, where I used to spend my time,
>   A-serving of her majesty, the Queen—
>   Of all them black-faced crew
>   The finest man I knew
>   Was our regimental bhisti, Gunga Din!"

She stopped for a second to gauge my reaction. I was kind of stunned that she could even go that far. I don't think I could recite two lines of poetry if you paid me. I've never really been able to concentrate on books—one page, and I'm off in la-la land. But there she was, orating away, gesturing with her arms, telling the tale with great flair. When she reached the end, she recited the last lines with so much emotion, it was like she was going to break down—

> "Though I've belted you and flayed you
>   By the living God that made you
>   You're a better man than I am, Gunga Din!"

I expected her to be beaming with pride when she finished, but she just gave a little bow, like it was nothing, and sat back down. I told her I didn't understand all of the story, and like a schoolteacher, she broke it down for me—explaining what a bhisti was, who Rudyard Kipling was, and what the fighting was about. She told me what some of the foreign words meant. It was all so exciting for me. I guess I just never really got that poem, when I was a kid in school—or most any poem, for that matter—but now for the first time I really wanted to learn, really wanted to know what it was all about.

A few nights later, I was clicking around the television when I saw Cary Grant yelling, "Din! Din!" And well, wouldn't you know it, it was the movie version of "Gunga Din." I wondered, what were the odds of that happening? I don't think I would have given that movie a second look if it wasn't for Edith. But because of her I was able to figure out what was going on. I mean, what did I know about these British sergeants and their native water bearer before Edith recited the poem to me? But now it was a lot clearer, and I could understand the honor, the glory, and the sacrifice that was being portrayed in this movie. I may have even understood Edith a little more, too.

The movie stayed with me. I don't know why, because as I said, I've never had what you would call a close personal relationship with books, but the next time I was at Edith's I borrowed her Kipling book and took it home. I wanted to learn the poem and recite it for her. I tried, for a week, to memorize little bits of it every night. I tried to remember the way she'd said it, because I knew if I didn't get it quite right she'd stop and correct me—"No, no, you have to emphasize it *this* way," I imagined her telling me.

I don't know why I felt this need to impress her. Other than, maybe, that she had impressed me so much. Here she was, eighty-five now, and still sharp as a tack. And so filled with emotion, and so many stories. I wanted to hear more of them. I wanted to know more about her.

So there it was. I was getting pulled more and more into Edith's life, and I hadn't really noticed it happening. You just do a little more, and a little more, and without realizing it you've turned a corner and can't go back. But what I don't think I realized at the time was how intrigued I was. I don't know if she did it on purpose, but Edith had a way of doling out information, just a little bit at a time, just enough to draw you in, to make you want to know a little more. The more I got to know her, the more I came to realize that of course she was doing it on purpose. Nothing, and I mean nothing, Edith did was by accident.

A few days later, I went over to take her to the doctor, and when I walked in, she was watching a movie on the VCR. It was a black-and-white movie; there on the screen, Mickey Rooney and Judy Garland were doing a dance number.

"What movie you watching, Edith?"

"Oh, this is *Girl Crazy*. That's little Mickey. I used to teach him, you know."

Yeah, right, is what I thought, but what I said was, "Oh, really?"

"Yes, he was much younger then, of course. I used to help him with his choreography. Nice boy. Very polite."

I decided to let it go. I was a few minutes early, so I sat down and started watching the movie with her. Just then, a band came on, and started playing a song I knew—"I Got Rhythm."

"That's Tommy," Edith said. Tommy Dorsey.

"No kidding?" I said. "Hey, Edith, you don't still have that saxophone around, do you?"

"No," she said, and now I was starting to feel a little more skeptical again, but of course I didn't say anything, and she continued. "The arrangement was, I was just going to hold it for him for a while, and when he had the money he would pay me back and I would return his saxophone to him. I don't know why, but I guess we both just forgot about it. I never gave it back to him. I finally sold it, about seven or eight years ago."

I wasn't sure what to make of all that. Did she have that movie on for my benefit, so she'd have an excuse to tell those stories? Or had she just happened to be in the mood to watch that particular movie? The way she told those stories, it wasn't as though she was trying to impress me. And her whole way of changing the subject if you pushed her on them too much: Was that because she was making them up and was afraid that if you asked too many questions she'd get caught in a lie? Or was it the opposite—were the stories a little too real for her, the past a little too close behind?

I had no idea. Anyway, the movie was just about wrapping up, and it was getting on time to go.

It was tougher than usual to get Edith up and out of the house that particular day. For some reason, she was moving very slowly. She had arthritis, and I thought maybe that was acting up. But she also had a big ganglion cyst on her elbow, which is what the appointment was for that day. I'd heard the treatment was pretty painful, that after the doctor drains the cyst he shoots you up with cortisone. Edith didn't seem to me to be the type that would be afraid of needles, but she seemed reticent to leave, getting distracted by one thing or another as I kept trying to get her out the door.

When we finally got to the doctor's office, she was even more obstinate. Edith had an old wheelchair lying around that I had brought with us, and I suggested that we use it. First she snapped that she didn't need a wheelchair—what did I take her for, some old cripple?—and then she started snapping at me because I wasn't getting the wheelchair ready fast enough.

By the time we got to the waiting room she was really impatient. I couldn't get her to chat. I couldn't get her to pick up a magazine and pass the time. After just a few minutes, she said, way too loud, "Let's just go. I don't want to stay here."

I tried to stay calm, because I thought that would keep her calm. I said, "Edith, we've gotten this far, we've come all the way down here, let's just wait and see the doctor."

"I had an appointment at eleven o'clock! It's way after eleven. If they can't keep their appointments then neither can I. Let's get the hell out of here!"

The women behind the counter weren't paying any attention to Edith—I guess they were used to this sort of thing—but the other people in the waiting room were all staring.

"Edith, you need to calm down," I said. "You're making a scene."

I guess that was the wrong thing to say. She started yelling at me, like she'd never yelled at me before. "Who the hell do you think you are," she hollered, "that you can tell me what to do? You don't know the first thing about anything, so shut your damn mouth and let's go!"

I was frozen. I didn't have the first clue how to handle this. Fortunately, right at that moment, one of the women behind the counter showed up next to us. I guess they were listening, after all.

"Mrs. Macefield?" she said, as though nothing out of the ordinary was going on. "Would you come with me? The doctor will see you now."

"Why, thank you, my dear," Edith said, calm as day. "You're very kind."

The young woman wheeled her toward the doctor's office, and I trailed behind, scratching my head.

Well, I sure have seen a lot of Ediths this morning, I thought. The one who taught dancing to Mickey Rooney. Or didn't. The one who bought Tommy Dorsey's saxophone because he needed money. Or didn't. The mean one, the crotchety one, the pleasant one, the angry one, the elegant one. Which of those was the real Edith, I wondered.

I'd find out soon enough: they all were.

7

Edith had been worrying me lately. She didn't seem to be eating breakfast unless I was there to get her up and going, and she was looking a little thinner than usual. Maybe it was just me being nervous, but either way, I started hinting that I could make breakfast for her. I'm pretty handy around the kitchen, and everybody seems pleased with my cooking.

But pleasing everybody and pleasing Edith were two different things.

Edith always had the same thing for breakfast, something she called sloppy toast. And she was very particular about the way it was prepared. Apparently the way you make sloppy toast is you toast bread, then you boil water, then you fry an egg. You pour the boiling water on the toast and then press down on it with a spatula to squish the water out of it. Then you lather it up with butter and put the eggs on top.

She just ignored me, the first couple of times I offered to make breakfast, but the third time she kind of just snorted and said, "Like you could ever figure out how to make sloppy toast."

I got her to let me give it a whirl anyway. The first time I made it, she just looked at it and said, "Hmm, not quite sure what to make of that." The second time it was "No, that's not quite it." Eventually, though, I got the hang of it to Edith's satisfaction.

So now I was there just about every morning for breakfast, and pretty soon it was every lunchtime, too. On days I was particularly busy I'd try to send one of the men to get her lunch—she was pretty addicted to that Big 'N Tasty and the vanilla shake by now—but she was just too ornery for them. I had two guys working for me called Big Eddie and Little Ed, and I sent Little Ed over there one time, and I guess she just ground him up and spit him out and said something like "Tell Barry not to send his goddamn lackey over here, you little twerp!" So Little Ed was actually afraid to go back over there. Once in a while Big Eddie would volunteer, but most of the time I went on my own. It was just easier that way.

And to be honest, it was more fun, too. Edith always had something to say about everything. It was around this time that Obama burst onto the national scene. She didn't particularly have anything against him, she just thought he wasn't old and experienced enough. But she liked him more than most of the other candidates out there. I could always push Edith's buttons and get her going, for example, just by mentioning John McCain's name. She thought that if he became president we'd be fighting everyone in the world.

She thought Sarah Palin was a joke altogether. "The

woman is just a showpiece," Edith said, waving a hand in dismissal. "She's just there for splash. She's outspoken, so they think she'll get them the women's votes. Like we're that dumb."

Sometimes, she'd just dismiss them all. "They're all a bunch of fools," she'd say. "Fortunately, it doesn't matter because the president is just a figurehead, the person in charge of hiring the smart people who really make things happen."

She was against the war in Iraq, as well. She knew more about how and why we got involved in it than I did, that's for sure. In fact, I didn't know anyone else who was so engaged in—well, engaged in just about everything. Funny, for a lady who didn't leave her house much, she sure was in touch with what was going on in the world. And I didn't know anyone else who knew as much about so many different topics, either. One day we were watching a show on PBS about the Three Tenors. I never would have watched it, but Edith kind of pulled me into it. She started by telling me how there were just a few true tenors in the world, and how these were considered the three best. As we were watching she pointed out when they were really hitting the note and when they weren't, when they fell a little short, and why the music was doing what it did in certain places. It was fascinating. More than that, it was amazing to me that I was fascinated by something I couldn't have given two shakes about before I sat down with Edith. Of course, I was half expecting her to tell me that Pavarotti was her first husband's cousin, or something like that, but that hadn't come up. Not so far, anyway.

When it was over, I asked her if there was any modern

music she liked. I was pretty shocked by who she came up with: Roy Orbison. But then I thought about it—he's kind of operatic in his own way, so I can understand that. The next day I brought over a Roy Orbison CD and we listened to some of that. I tried a Van Morrison CD, too, but she wasn't having any of it. "There isn't any direction to that music," she sniffed, and that was that.

A little while later, Edith was fussing around with some papers in a box on her desk, and she pulled out a photo and handed it to me. "This is my mother," she said. "I don't think I ever showed you her picture before."

I looked at the photo. Even though it was probably thirty years ago or more, I recognized Edith right away. She was sitting at a picnic table across from a woman who seemed awfully dour, although maybe it was just the blank expression that people of her generation seemed to put on in front of a camera, like that painting of a farmer and his wife with the pitchfork. There were what looked like some tents behind them.

Edith's relationship with her mother always seemed kind of odd to me. Edith was devoted to her—she'd given up everything to come back to America to take care of her—and yet some of the stories I'd heard were so strange. Once, Edith told me that her mother had gotten angry at her as a girl, and dragged her across the room by her hair. I got the impression that Edith did everything she could to please her mother, but much of it seemed to have the opposite effect.

"Where was this photo taken, Edith?" I asked.

"It was at that cabin we had up in the woods," she said. "My mother loved that cabin. But that photo is from before it was actually built."

Edith had mentioned it once before: She and her mother owned some land up on the South Fork of the Stillaguamish River, about an hour north of Ballard. There wasn't much fishing on the South Fork, but they weren't the fishing type, from the sound of things. They'd started going there for picnics, and had planted some fruit trees. At some point, they built a little one-room cabin on the property.

"We spent a lot of time up there," Edith was saying now. "My mother liked to sit and look at the river. I used to like to write there. I put in a big mailbox so the magazines could send my rejection notices there," she said with a smile.

I took another look at the photo. Maybe it wasn't as dour as I thought. Funny how you can look at the same picture twice and see two different things.

"It was good of you to come back to America and take care of her, the way you did," I said, handing the photo back to her.

Edith took it, and put it back in the shoe box it came from, and gave me kind of a blank stare. "Of course I took care of her," she said. "What else would a person do?"

It had been a little more than a year since we first broke ground. The construction project was settling into a pretty regular routine now; the guys who worked for me knew what they were doing, so it wasn't hard for me to meet with them, figure out the plan for the next couple of hours, then get out of their hair so they could do their jobs. Our team was getting pretty efficient, and I think it helped me feel less guilty about the amount of time I was spending over at Edith's.

One afternoon when I walked in to check on her, she was watching *Lawrence of Arabia* on TV. When I sat down to watch with her, she said, "You know, I lived for a while in Africa, at that oasis not too far from where all this took place." She just mentioned it, and then let it drop. I tried to get a little more out of her, but she didn't respond. Later that same evening we turned on Lawrence Welk, and in the middle of it she pointed to the screen, where they were showing a wide shot of the band. "Hey, I think that's my uncle Eddy!" she said. A few seconds later, the camera panned back to the same wide shot. "That is my uncle Eddy! Playing the trumpet." She seemed delighted with herself for noticing. Again, I asked her about it, but she just pretended not to hear. So, that's how you'd learn that Edith had an uncle who played in Lawrence Welk's band, or that she lived on an oasis in Africa (if, in fact, any of that was true). The information would surface, suddenly, and then disappear again.

These were the little things that started making up who we were—TV, and music, and little snippets of her past. And the books, of course. She loved to talk about books, although that was the hardest for me. One day while we were waiting for her dinner to cook, Edith started explaining *Moby-Dick* to me—talk about feeling like a schoolkid. She described it as a kind of symbol; some people said it was a symbol of man searching for God, but she thought of it as a symbol of man fighting against what he believed was total evil, and I thought, well, that's a whole different book than the one I read in school.

Or, to be honest, the one they tried to get me to read in school. I sure never got through it. Getting through that book, for me, would have been harder than catching the whale itself.

There was a book about Hitler that I noticed on the shelf one evening, and I asked her if she'd read it. "I've read them all," she snapped. "Why would you have a book and not read it?"

I lobbed a question out there, knowing full well it would blow up like a grenade right in my face. "So, Edith, did you really spy on the Nazis?"

Much to my surprise, this time she didn't bat an eye. She started telling me an incredible tale.

What she told me was that she had met Hitler. Several times.

Hitler was gathering up singers and artists for big parties right around the time she arrived in Germany, Edith told me. She was masquerading as a music student and was a pretty good clarinet player, and wound up getting herself invited to those parties. At one of them, Hitler brought over a young blond boy. He never said so, but Edith believed he was Hitler's son. Later, Edith said, he would ask her to take care of the boy.

I was dumbstruck. "So, what happened? Did you? What happened to the boy?" I asked.

"Oh, you know how these things go," she said. Well, no, I sure didn't know.

But I guess, on this afternoon, I wasn't going to find out.

• • •

I'm surprised the school bell didn't ring every time I walked into Edith's house; that's how much of a schoolteacher she was. No matter what I was doing, she presented it as a challenge I had to master. For example, she got to the point where she couldn't operate the scissors to cut the liners for her false teeth, so I offered to do it for her. Immediately, she went into teacher mode, like she was Yoda and I was trying to cut the liners using The Force.

It wasn't exactly rocket science, and a guy who was in charge of building a shopping mall ought to be able to put a little liner into someone's false teeth. So I just jumped right in. But when I handed them to her, she said, "Oh no, that's not right at all. For goodness sakes, can't you get anything right?" And I just told her I'd try again, and imagined her saying, like Yoda, "Do or do not. There is no try."

So the next time, it was "No, this doesn't fit right," and then "Well, that's a little better," and then finally, "Oh, that looks pretty good—hey, you're better at this than me." Now all of a sudden I was the full-time tooth-liner man, and feeling good about it to boot, because I'd pleased the teacher.

As I said, I think Edith always knew exactly what she was doing.

It was around this time that the mall was actually starting to rise up from the ground. The foundation was finished, and when you walked by you'd see the rebar sticking up from it. (*Rebar* is short for reinforcing bar, those things that look like spiraled metal sticks that poke up from the ground at construction sites.) We were encasing the rebar in concrete, and soon the site looked like a bunch of crisscrossed concrete gap-toothed combs. Laying the bottom of the first floor on those concrete columns—the floor itself being a concrete slab—is a little tricky. To the casual observer, concrete is inflexible, but in reality, it's quite alive; it flexes and moves and bends, and if you're going to have a building that doesn't fall apart you have to get the dynamic tension into the slab. So you build what will look like the floor, but you make it out of plywood, and you lay long cables through it, along with some more rebar. When you pour the concrete over that plywood floor, the cables and the rebar become encased in it, and the blue cables stick out of the ends, so you can pull on those cables with a special machine that puts exactly the right tension on the cable. Anyway, all of that gives the concrete the strength to stay up there and not crack and fall. And now you've got one floor built. You go up ten feet, and start the process all over again for the second floor.

The walls themselves are made separately. You make forms reinforced with rebar where the walls are going to be. When you pour the concrete and it hardens, you strip off the forms, and lo and behold, there stand the walls. It's all a matter of strength. Nothing stands on its own, but if it has the right structure, properly formed and correctly reinforced, it can withstand just about anything and not move an inch.

Not so different from Edith, when you come to think about it.

It was around that time that I got the first call from Edith's social workers. Edith had told me they'd been coming by, asking her what day of the week it was and who the president is and such. She was kind of bemused by all of that, when she wasn't outright pissed off. And I guess Edith must have told them that I was watching out for her, or something, because they called me up, and after some initial chitchat they got to the point: They didn't think she was capable of staying in the house by herself. Could I help convince her to move?

It was pretty clear they didn't know much about Edith.

They didn't know much about me, either.

They said she couldn't live by herself, because what if something happened? And I said, well, something could happen anywhere. I was just thirty seconds away, and I would keep checking on her. They told me, "Well, if something goes wrong, you're going to be responsible."

At that, something welled up inside of me, something I hadn't felt before. I think it was the first time I really understood what Edith was trying to teach me. Because when I responded, I sounded a lot more like Edith than I did like myself.

"How the heck am I responsible?" I said, probably just a little too loudly. "I'll check on her and all, but she's a grown woman, and she can make her own decisions. She's eighty-five years old and she's perfectly capable of understanding what she can and cannot do. If she decides she wants to take that risk because it means staying in her own house, well, then that's her right. People have rights, you know."

I was kind of surprised to hear all that come out of me, but it's like ringing a bell. Once it's out there, it's out there. You can't unring it.

What happened next came pretty fast. Edith got a visit from her estate lawyer—I'm guessing the social workers put him up to it—who told her she needed to give someone power of attorney. She just turned to me and said, "Well, I guess you're it." "I'm what?" I asked her. "My power of attorney."

A few weeks later, I had to take Edith to the hospital again. I don't want to go into too much detail, but let's just say she was having some problems with her plumbing. Afterward, she was at a rehab center for a while, and the folks there also talked to me about the power-of-attorney question, and when I told them what Edith had said, they offered to help me get the paperwork together. I think it was a couple of days later that Charlie stopped by for a visit, and happened to be in the room when the rehab administrative assistant came in and asked me how the paperwork for the power of attorney was coming.

He seemed to be pretty perturbed. "What kind of power of attorney are you looking for, exactly?" he snapped. "I'm not looking for anything," I snapped right back. I was getting a little tired of this guy by now, to tell you the truth. He hadn't been in the picture much at all lately, but now here he was getting his hackles up about the details of Edith's legal standing.

It wasn't until Edith got back home from the hospital that things started falling into place for me.

Now that I had filled out the papers to get her power of attorney, she started handing me big manila folders filled with papers. One of them had her will, and when I read it, I just about fell over.

It said that if Edith were ever declared incompetent, then Charlie would take over her estate.

So that made me awful suspicious. I started piecing together why Charlie might have gotten so angry at Edith for not taking the million dollars—the million dollars that could have easily wound up falling right in his lap, if someone decided she couldn't make her own decisions anymore.

I could never be certain—but there was one thing I was certain about.

Edith was going to stay in her house. And I was going to make sure of it.

So I guess, in a way, those social workers were right after all.

I had decided to become responsible.

8

As the days got shorter that fall, I had given up all pretense that there was some separation between my life with Edith and my life without. I wasn't spending the weekends with her, but when I wasn't in the construction trailer I was in that house from dawn till way after dark, making all of Edith's meals, taking care of the bills and the lawn and the chores, the shopping and the laundry, and sitting and watching TV with her most of the day. The TV was on constantly—I never lived like that, but I got so used to it that on the odd occasion when I'd come in and the TV wasn't on, it felt like something was seriously amiss.

Edith was pretty much living just on the first floor now. Ever since the last time she fell, she didn't try to make it up the stairs anymore. I had put a little commode next to the couch, and sometimes I'd be at the trailer and the phone would ring. "I left you a little present," Edith would say, with almost a hint of a giggle, and I'd walk the twenty-nine steps back over to her house—I counted it once just for fun, and the number stuck in my head—and go clean out the commode.

It's stunning, I guess, when I think about how easily Evie took to all this. When your husband's gone all day for work, that's one thing; but when he's gone for most of the evening, too, taking care of someone he's not even related to, someone you've met only once or twice, well, that takes someone pretty special. Occasionally she'd get irritated, of course. On the odd chance I'd make it home before dark, as often as not Edith would call on my cell phone with some problem or other, some excuse to make me drive back there. I had an accident, she'd say, or you forgot to leave water for me—I swear, she'd take that pitcher of water I left on the table and struggle her way over to the sink to dump it out, just to get me to come back—anything to make me get my sorry butt back in the truck and drive the forty-five minutes back to her place. So on nights when we had plans to be with our friends or do something with the kids, and I'd have to pick up and drive over to Edith's, well, that burned Evie a bit. I could always tell when she was a little steamed. The cell phone would ring—I had a separate ring tone for Edith—and Evie would hear it and say, "Oh my god, here we go again." Because it would happen a lot. Or we'd be sitting down to dinner and the phone would ring and she'd say, "Maybe you ought to just have dinner over there already." It was understandable that she'd get a little peeved. When you've got two teenagers at home, there's always too much for one person to do. My kids are good and all, but any parent will admit that those years are an ordeal, even with the best of teenagers.

But when I asked Evie about it, all she'd ever say was that she was proud of me. "It takes a special person to do this," she said one night. I knew she knew how much it took. Her mother had died not too long ago, and Evie had been the caregiver, as she had for her dad years before that. When Evie said that to me, I flashed on my own mom. I'd forgotten, but there was a well-known architect my dad had done work for. When the architect got old, my mom became his caregiver. When he died, his wife took ill, and then my mom became her caregiver as well. I've thought all my life about what my dad has passed on to me—but maybe this is another kind of family tradition. A good one, too.

"It's good that you're doing this," Evie told me. "People don't just do this, you know."

"We do," I said, and she knew what I meant.

It had been a year and a half since I first met Edith. I'd finally gotten the power-of-attorney thing straightened out, and the first thing she wanted to do was reconfigure her will. She was anxious to get it done, she said, because Charlie was still in the will, and she explained—with a good number of profanities attached to his name—that she wanted him out of there.

She wanted to leave everything to me.

I was stunned by that. It was touching, but it was also

embarrassing. It made me uncomfortable. For one, I didn't think I was deserving. For another, there were enough people out there thinking I had some ulterior motive for helping to take care of Edith, without giving them any fuel for their fire.

But it was what she said she wanted, so I told her I'd contact the lawyer and get the ball rolling. Truth be told, though, I stalled off for a long time. I figured maybe she's just mad at Charlie, so I'll give her some time to change her mind back. I didn't need anyone thinking I was a money-grubber and I didn't particularly relish the idea of putting my name in Edith's will, so I just let it sit for a bit.

I managed to stay home most of the weekend, although that was getting trickier and trickier, too. I had a little platoon of helpers who would look in on Edith: Mike up at Mike's Chili, and her friend Gail who came by to visit, and one or two others. I had all their numbers in my phone, and when I had to, I'd give one of them a call and have them bring her a meal or check in on her and report back to me. Charlie was still coming by to visit every once in a while, too, although those visits became less and less frequent. It got to the point where months would go by without a word from him.

Edith was still more capable of taking care of herself than I probably gave her credit for. But I was learning. I was learning, as the days were getting shorter, just how much of the stuff we do for old people we do to make ourselves feel better, or to make things easier for ourselves. We don't always listen to what they're trying to tell us. I learned that every time Edith swatted my hands away when I'd try to help her wipe her mouth or tie a shoelace. One evening I had made her one of her Stouffer's frozen mac-and-cheese dinners, and I saw her struggling to eat it. Her arthritis was so bad by now that she couldn't really rotate her wrist, so she'd bring a forkful of it up to her mouth, and it would keep falling off. I swear more of it wound up in her lap than in her mouth. I figured it would be easier if I helped her do it, so I reached over to take the fork, and she slapped my hand, as hard as she could (which was surprisingly hard, considering). "I can do it myself!" she roared at me. This happened a few times before I finally realized that it was the same thing you do with a child. You try to convince them to let you help them, not for their sake, but for your own, just to get through the day a little more quickly. So when you realize that what you're doing is for your own sake and not theirs it kind of stops you. If you can take a breath and step back, and say, well, okay, go ahead and do it for yourself, I'm not stopping you—it might make a few tasks go more slowly, but it does help you achieve a kind of harmony together. And I guess it allows them to hang on to a little bit of their dignity.

Dignity's a hard thing to let go of, especially for someone who has lived the kind of life Edith apparently had—sometimes glamorous, sometimes dangerous, always exciting. So when it gets to the point where you've got to do your business in a commode and have someone clean it out for you, that's got to be difficult.

Edith handled it as best as you can expect. One day she

asked me to help her take a bath, and from the expression on
my face she guessed I was pretty embarrassed at the idea. But
she just said, "Well, sweetheart, if you haven't seen a pair of
boobs by now you've got a long way to go, and if these old
sagging ones excite you there's something wrong with you.
So I suggest we get to it." Just like that—as matter-of-factly as
if she was asking me to hand her a handkerchief. So as I said,
I guess she was handling it as well as anyone could.

Little by little, I learned where the limits were. The next
time I saw her struggling to eat her mac and cheese, I didn't
say a word. Edith could pound the food away like a sailor—
she could eat more than I could—but now she was getting ex-
hausted by the effort but was still hungry. I was watching for
when she reached that point, and when I figured she had, I
asked, politely, "Now, Edith, here, do you want me to help
you with the rest of that?" and waited for the explosion. But it
never came. She just said, "Well, thank you, Barry, yes, that
would be helpful."

I thought carefully about the difference between our two
mac-and-cheese incidents, and all I could come up with was
that the first time, I took control of the situation away from
her, and the second time, I left her in control. It was her decision to allow me to help her. I was always a slow learner, but
I think I was finally beginning to catch on.

And yet, as much as it was a relief to see that Edith and I
were getting to a place where we understood each other—or
understood each other better, at least—the pain and sleepless-
ness Edith was struggling with were getting worse. I didn't
seem to be of much help there. I took her to doctors a lot that

fall to try to figure out what the pain was all about. I think there was a part of her that didn't really want to know, because I'd schedule all these CAT scans and X-rays and such, and right down to fifteen minutes before we were supposed to go, when I'd have her all dressed and everything, she'd say, "I've changed my mind. I'm not going. Those doctors don't know what they're doing anyway. It's a waste of my time."

Once in a while, if it was something particularly important, I'd fight her on it; but as I said, I'd learned a lot by now about doing things to ease your own guilt versus doing things to help the person you're supposed to be helping. She was still an adult and still able to make her own decisions. If I was going to say Charlie was wrong about her being incompetent, then I had to put my money where my mouth was and give her a chance to do what she wanted, even if some guy from the construction site next door thought it was a bad decision. She might not have been able to take a bath on her own anymore, but she could at least do that.

I never ate dinner with Edith during that fall. That was one way I was trying to preserve my own little shrinking corner of a private life. No matter how late it was, I'd get Edith settled on the couch, and then go home for dinner with Evie and the kids. It was nice that they always waited dinner for me. I'd call Evie when I was out the door and around the corner, so she could time her cooking. We ate a lot of fish, or a tenderloin from Costco, and always a lot of fresh vegetables. It was always important to us to have a good dinner for the family and to eat together whenever we could, just to catch up on each other's day. Willy was pretty oblivious when it came to Edith, but Kelsey would ask about her a lot. Willy was busy with his senior project then; he thought he might want to be an architect, so for his project he was designing and building a trellis. I acted like his contractor on the job, and treated him like the architect: I told him I needed drawings to scale, top view and side view, and then I helped him build it. Kelsey had started community college, and was struggling a little with math; I kept encouraging her to take advantage of the tutors and the other resources they had available for her. She resisted for a little while, but then she took them up on it, and that was helping.

To get home for dinner, though, I had a whole elaborate routine to get through. After I finished up with the guys at the site, I'd go cook Edith's dinner. Those frozen dinners she ate when Charlie was buying her groceries seemed like a pretty crummy thing to live on, so I tried to make dinner a little more interesting and healthy—some fresh fish and a vegetable or two, something like that. A little more like the way we ate at home.

While she'd eat, I'd do the day's dishes. She'd feed herself until she couldn't anymore, then—asking permission first—I'd help her with the rest of her dinner. After that we'd get the coffee table next to the couch set up for the night. Everything had to be in exactly the right place. A box of tissues at one end (and there had better be enough tissues in the box, or I'd hear about it plenty). Next to that a water cup, and under the table some containers with water and ice, so she'd have cold water all night. I'd have to place them just so, so that she could reach them without knocking them over. I'd put the little commode at the end of the coffee table by the head of the couch, so she could sit up and grab the handles and pull herself over onto it. I'd make sure there was plenty of toilet paper nearby. Next to the water cup I put a little pillbox with her sleeping pills. She told me she had been waking up every two hours like clockwork; I would leave just enough of the sleeping pills to get her through the night. That was one of the arguments I didn't let her win. If I let her have her pillbox, she'd sometimes forget what she'd taken and wind up taking too many. Or she'd try to open it herself and there'd be 150 pills on the floor. So this was one time when I decided her safety had to win out over her dignity, and I put my foot down.

She didn't like that one bit.

Once the table was set up, I'd give her dessert—some milk and cookies or ice cream. She'd select five CDs for me to put in the changer. The first was always Richard Tauber, her supposed husband. The violins would swell, and this very formal voice with a sort of German accent would come on. I'd never heard anything quite like it before. It seemed kind of like opera to me, stuffy and stiff at first, rising and powerful in the middle, then very tender and almost tearful at the end. It was like watching a whole play being performed in a few minutes. From the first notes, Edith seemed to relax in a way she hadn't all day. A little smile would come onto her face, and as the lyrics began—"Without a song, the day would never end"—I'd lean over and kiss her on the forehead, and say good night.

One night, after I did, she reached over and took my arm, something she never did. In a voice that was much softer than I was used to from Edith, she said, "Barry, you know, my mother never kissed me."

I wasn't sure what to say in response to that. I just patted her arm and turned to go. Richard Tauber was reaching his tender finale—"I only know there ain't no love at all, without a song"—as I turned the key to lock the door behind me, and walked slowly to my truck.

I knew it wasn't easy for Edith to express her feelings. Not like she had that night. It's one of those things you adjust to, when you're taking care of an older person—what level of openness they're used to. Edith clearly wasn't used to much, which was fine with me. I like to let actions speak louder than words anyway, and I guess Edith was the same—odd, considering she was a writer, but that's what it was. So when I'd leave, sometimes she'd give me a hard time, and I'd say, in a joking way, "You'd better watch out or I'll come over there and knock your walker out from under you, old woman," and she'd smile, and I think that was the level of affection that both of us were comfortable with. Or that Mother's Day, she gave me some jewelry that she wanted Evie to have, and I said, "Well, that's really nice, Edith. Make sure to answer the phone when it rings"—sometimes Edith just ignored it—"because that'll be Evie calling you to say thanks." And Edith said, "Oh, no no no, I don't want it to be coming from me. I want it to be coming from you."

So that was the way Edith expressed her affection, or her thanks. A kind of side-door approach to love is how I thought of it. That night at dinner I gave Evie the jewelry; I told her where it came from, of course, and I repeated what Edith had said, and how she couldn't call and say thanks. "For an ornery old woman, she's pretty sweet," Evie said. I thought that was a pretty good assessment.

Sweet or not, Edith was digging her heels in, which meant that my dinners with Evie and the kids were being threatened. Edith was making it harder and harder for me to leave. One night, as I was walking out the door and Richard Tauber was singing about how a man is born but he's no good no-how without a song, Edith suddenly collapsed on the floor. "I can't breathe!" she said. "I'm dying! I can't breathe!"

I panicked for a second, but when I looked at her skin it was perfectly flush, so I could see she was getting plenty of oxygen. I squeezed her finger to make sure—I learned somewhere along the line that if you squeeze someone's finger and the red color comes back immediately, they're getting enough oxygen, but if they're not, the color won't come back. So I knew she was fine. "Edith, it's just your anxiety. You're okay," I'd say to her, but I'd have to stay until she calmed down.

About half the time, I wouldn't get home before Edith would call on the cell. I'd forgotten the pills, she'd say, or I can't reach the water, or the CD player had stopped working. Something—anything—to drag me back. I'd have to call Evie and say, "I'm at the floating bridge, and Edith just called. You guys have dinner without me. Sorry."

I resisted Edith's ploys as much as I could, but it was getting harder and harder.

Because now she had started sleepwalking.

She swore she wasn't, but she couldn't explain why some mornings I would come in and find her across the room, bare naked in the middle of the floor. A couple of times, she'd wake up and not be able to get back to the couch—once she was down, she couldn't get back up—but she could reach the phone, so she'd call me at two or three in the morning. Or she'd call the fire department, and they'd come bust in. I can't remember how many times I had to rebuild that doorjamb.

It was really starting to wear on me. Remember that in the middle of all this I was in charge of a multimillion-dollar project. Everyone was counting on me, and suddenly I'm showing up half asleep because I was up in the middle of the night driving back to help Edith off the floor.

So now it had gotten to the point where I was either going to stay there all night—not an option for me—or get some help.

Apparently, not an option for Edith.

I called an outfit called Helping Hands, which helps to provide home care. The first woman they sent out looked pretty promising. Edith liked her, maybe because she seemed to innately understand the difference between doing things to help Edith, which was okay, and doing things *for* Edith, which she bristled at. I was feeling pretty proud of myself for getting the home care in place. I even let myself imagine the luxury of having more time with my family.

Think again, Barry Martin.

When I showed up the next morning, the woman told me she'd had to lift Edith off the floor a few times in the night, and the lifting was too much for her.

So I was back to square one.

They kept sending over new people, and Edith managed to find something wrong with each one of them. One was a college student, sweet as pie, I thought, but the first moment she could, Edith said to me, "Get that bitch out of here." The next gal I got, she was too lazy for Edith. "She just watches TV all night and the TV keeps me awake!" Edith complained. Never mind that she had the stereo or the TV on all night anyway.

I thought we'd reached some kind of détente, I guess they call it, when the next gal showed up. She was a little older and seemed more patient with the ways of elderly people. She told me she was used to older people being kind of cranky. But I don't think she'd ever come up against anyone as ornery as Edith.

The first night, as I was giving the woman her instructions, Edith suddenly collapsed on the floor. "I can't breathe!" she called out. "I'm dying! I can't breathe!"

The woman's eyes were wide. I could tell she was totally freaked out. "Edith," I said, "with all the lives you led, are you sure you were never an actress? Because you're putting on quite a show right now."

It didn't take Edith long to calm down, but I don't think that woman could get out of the house fast enough.

The next day, I had a little heart-to-heart with Edith.

"You know, I don't think you're going to let anyone come in," I said flat out.

"Well, if you'd stop bringing in these incompetents, maybe we could get somewhere," she shot back. But I could tell she was wondering where I was going with this.

"Well, if you're going to keep having these emergencies at night, and you won't let anybody stay here, then we're going to have to make a change," I said. She didn't ask me what I meant by that and I didn't elaborate, but I could tell I'd gotten her attention.

I told her that I'd give up on trying to get help for the moment, but only if she'd meet me halfway in trying to solve some of these supposed disasters in the night.

I think she understood that she had reached a certain limit with me, because suddenly, most of the problems went away. No more panic calls at night. No more I-can't-breathe.

When I look back on it, I think Edith was testing me again—testing to find out what my limit was. Whether I'd stick with her when times got tough, and just how far I was willing to go. This is a woman who, if her stories are to be believed, managed to outfox the Nazis; I guess I shouldn't be surprised that she was able to outfox a middle-aged construction superintendent. She'd gotten her way—we weren't going to hire any help, at least for now—but I'd put an end to her demands. For the moment.

We managed to cure the sleepwalking as well. It was right around this time that stories started coming out in the press about people sleepwalking on sleeping pills. I did a little homework, and figured out that the different kinds of sleeping pills—Ambien and the generic version, straight capsules and time-release—might have different effects. I insisted that the pharmacy switch her to a different version of the drug she was taking, just to see if it worked. Sure enough, it did the trick. Edith was sleeping through the night, and I went back to having dinner with my wife.

That first night she was on the new pills, though, I decided to stay after Edith went to sleep, just to be safe. Once she'd drifted off, I noticed a book on the shelf.

It was *Moby-Dick*.

I knew I'd still never get through it all, but after all of our conversations, I decided to crack the cover. I got as far as the first sentence. "Call me Ishmael," it started. Everybody knows that line, of course, but for the first time, it made me wonder—isn't that kind of a strange way to start a book? I mean, either the guy's name is Ishmael or it isn't, and if it isn't, and if he just wants you to call him that, why doesn't he want you to know who he really is?

I put the book down and decided that maybe tomorrow, in the light of day, I'd ask Edith about it.

9

Anyone who works in construction knows that whatever can go wrong on a job probably will. And if I was a betting man, I would have bet that if we were going to run into Murphy's Law, it would have something to do with the high-tension wires.

I had my history with high-tension wires, the ones you see suspended between utility poles. They're called high-tension wires because they're running 50,000 volts or more; they don't have insulation on them, so if you touch one, you're done. Kaput.

A few years back, I was working on building a sewage treatment plant near some of those high-tension wires. We had a special safety meeting about them because this one guy was working on a concrete pump truck pretty close to the wires. You had to keep all equipment at least ten feet away from the wires to make sure the electricity didn't arc over and zap you. Well, the concrete pump truck had a long boom on it, several stories high. The operator of the truck worked from the bottom of the boom, with a handheld remote control box that had a kind of umbilical cord that went back to the machine.

Over on the other side of the project, we were digging a deep ditch for a six-foot sewer pipe, and were about to lower a big metal box into the hole. The box is called a "coffin," which sounds ominous, but it's really a safety mechanism— a huge metal box, probably twenty feet long, of double-reinforced steel, that you lower into the hole while you're working down there. If the hole decides to cave in, you'll be protected inside that box.

Well, we had the giant coffin suspended over the hole, and were just getting ready to lower it when the cable that was holding it broke. You can't imagine the noise of this giant metal box dropping twenty feet down into this hole—it sounded like a bomb going off. It was a twenty-acre site that we were working on, but the noise reverberated across the whole site. When you hear something like that, you just know something really bad has happened. Everybody stopped what they were doing and turned to see what had gone wrong.

Unfortunately, the guy who was working the concrete pump was retracting his boom right at that very moment. He took his eyes off of what he was doing just for a second, the boom swung around, and it hit those high-tension wires dead on.

They tell me that blue flames shot out of his mouth when the power surge hit him. By the time I ran over, he was unconscious. I gave him CPR, pushing on his chest and breathing into his mouth, trying to will him to hang on to life, but there was no hope. He was probably dead the instant the electricity struck.

So as I said, I had a history with the high-tension wires, and when we started the mall project it was one of the first things that caught my attention. The owners had made the decision that those wires needed to go underground. It's a complex process, getting approval to move those wires. You have to fill out mounds of paperwork and get all sorts of city officials to sign off, and lay the proper conduit in the ground for the wires to be put into. So I was about as pissed off as can be, when I found out that the owners' civil engineer on the project hadn't started the process on time. We gave formal written notice to the owners that because they had neglected to get the wires moved, we were going to have to rearrange how we would proceed with the entire project. We were on the second floor now, and if I were to stand at the edge of the building I could reach out and touch the utility pole. If we went up one more floor, we'd be within ten feet of the high-tension wires.

So basically I had to start creating a kind of stair-step-shaped building up to the fifth floor—we built the floors up on one side of the project, and left the building just two stories tall on the north side by the wires, until everybody could get their act together and get the wires moved.

It was an enormous pain in the ass.

And it didn't make my life any easier that right at that moment the press was starting to get kind of out of hand, as well. The media attention had been just background noise for me ever since the project started. I didn't know it at the time, but that first column by Danny Westneat had been picked up by a nationally syndicated news column called "News of the Weird," which kind of made fun of Edith:

> The *Seattle Times* reported in February that Edith Macefield, 84, living in a tiny, rundown, 106-year-old house in an industrial neighborhood, across from a chemical plant, had rejected a final buyout offer from developers amounting to nearly $750,000. "I don't care about money," she said. "It's [been] my home [for 54 years now]. . . . What would I do with that kind of money anyway?" The developer has purchased the rest of the block and will build around her tiny lot, boxing her in with walls 60 feet high.

I guess that column kept the story on the national radar, because every once in a while we'd get a call from someone wanting to interview Edith. The local media kept on the story pretty much all the way along, but for the most part they were polite about it. Not always, of course. After the offering price on Edith's house had been raised to a million dollars, it seemed like every time there was a slow news day they'd come camp out again. I'd be sitting with Edith and she'd say, "Barry, there's a news crew outside again," and I'd look out and think, oh, shit. When I went out to go back to the trailer, they'd hound me like a rock star. I didn't talk to them much, because I didn't think there was any way I was going to change their minds. They decided we were the bad guys trying to squeeze this lady out of her house, and I couldn't think of anything I could say that would make them feel differently. Once in a while, I'd say, "You know, you've never talked to her, so how can you say how she's feeling or what she's thinking?"—but they'd just use that as an excuse to try to get me to land an interview with her. And Edith was having none of that.

It was around that time that a play called *Radio Golf* opened downtown at the Seattle Repertory Theater. I didn't go see it, but I sure heard about it. It was a play about a greedy development company that's building a big apartment complex in a run-down neighborhood, and all that's left on the property is one rickety old house. The person who lives in the house, some very colorful old character with interesting stories in his past, refuses to sell it. The press picked up on the coincidence between that play and our situation. Apparently, the guy in the play who's trying to preserve the house even does a sketch of the development that looks just like our plans, with a hole cut around the tiny house. Of course, in the play, the developer has no conscience; one character even compares the development to stealing land from Native Americans. "You're the cowboys. I'm the Indians," he says. "We'll see who wins this war." I'm told that in the end, one of the developers goes over to the side of the fellow who's trying to stay in his house. But that didn't get into the papers when they compared us to the play. They just wrote about "the moral tradeoffs of gentrification."

I started feeling like I was living in two different worlds. There was this public perception, in which Edith and I were part of some big play with big themes, a play about preserving the past and about the evils of progress. And then there was the day-to-day world, where it was just Edith and me, living our lives.

For the most part, the public brouhaha was just background rumble for us. Everybody was calling or sending letters—Jay Leno, Ellen DeGeneres—and Edith was just ignoring them. But it finally reached a peak in October 2007. That's when CBS News started calling.

The only person who had ever landed an interview with Edith was the original *Seattle Post-Intelligencer* reporter who wrote about the story back when it all began. A nice, well-mannered young woman, she had the good sense to call Edith "Miss Macefield," to show up dressed nicely and speak very politely. Edith turned her down the first few times she came around, but one day she opened the door, and said to the girl, "My, what a nice dress you have on; please, come in and have some tea."

But when Steve Hartman showed up to do his story for the evening news, cameras rolling, banging on the door and calling for her by her first name, she gave him what for. And that, unfortunately, became part of the story as well. The footage of Hartman calling, "Edith, any chance of an interview?" and Edith barking, "Go away!" became one of those Internet sensations. Within a few days, it seemed like everyone had seen it. Hartman had sent Edith flowers, and she gave them to me to take home to Evie. Every time I looked at them, I thought, well, if I'm going to be buried by the media, at least I've got some nice flowers for my grave.

I had given an interview to Hartman, trying to explain

how the relationship with Edith was very different from what the media was portraying. The next night, we watched ourselves on the evening news. They showed her little house, with the big mall walls already towering over it.

"Today, just two pickets on the fence separate Edith from the west wall," Hartman was saying in voice-over. "The north and east are closer still. She's got Porta-Potties doing fly-bys, and the noise—forget wind chimes. Aerosmith couldn't drown out this racket. When the job is done, Edith's house will be surrounded on three sides by five stories of cement. Why would anyone want to stay here?"

But to his credit, Hartman did seem to have a sense of why Edith would want to stay. "People who know Edith say she's not moving for three main reasons," he said over more images of the house. "First of all, she's lived here for more than forty years and has some great memories from those decidedly quieter times. Secondly, she doesn't want to have to move all her stuff; and finally, she's really gotten to like her new neighbors."

After that, they cut to a sound bite from me, and I thought, well, that ought to quiet things down. Finally, the national news was showing how Edith and I had become friends. Now, I thought, maybe the protesters would leave me alone.

Shows how much I know.

All the local media came barking around again. A local tattoo parlor created a tattoo of Edith's house, with the word *steadfast* underneath it. Whatever point Hartman was trying to make with that piece, the only effect it had was to reinforce for everybody what they already wanted to believe.

The next day, as I was leaving Edith's, I noticed two women walking toward me and pointing. They were what we used to call Granola Gals, kind of sixties leftovers—not at all unusual for Ballard—one tall and heavy and dressed in man's clothing, the other thin and short and wearing a long dress. They stopped when they got close to me.

"How dare you!" the tall one yelled at me.

I stopped and looked her in the eye.

"How dare I what?"

The two of them laid into me pretty good. "How could you do this to this poor old lady!" they screamed. "Don't you have any courtesy, any common sense, any decency? What is the matter with you! Why would you do this to someone!"

Well, I guess if I did have any common sense I might have just walked on, but something in me snapped. Sometimes you just have to say enough is enough, and stand up for yourself.

"Well, first off, this 'poor old woman' has a name. It's Edith Wilson Macefield." Edith had once told me that she always introduced herself with three names, that it's important for a woman to keep and carry her maiden name to maintain her identity, and I was proud of myself for remembering that in this moment. "That's Miss Macefield to you. Second, have you ever talked to her? Because if you did, you'd know nobody's doing anything to her."

They pushed their faces closer to mine, and yelled at me some more. I tried to keep my voice down, but I was getting pretty hot.

"Did you ever stop and talk to her? Are you here making

breakfast, lunch, and dinner for her, or driving her to her doctor appointments or making sure she has water next to her bed at night? Listen, she's still here, isn't she?"

"Right," the taller one shouted at me. Clearly, she was the one in charge of this little assault. "They did the same thing to us. We got forced out just like you're forcing that little old woman out."

"Nobody's forcing her out," I said. "They made her a decent offer, way more than decent, and she's still here. But you go ahead and believe what you want to believe. Don't let the facts get in your way."

With that, I pushed past them and headed to the construction trailer. They kept yelling at me as I walked, but they didn't follow me, and when I sat down at my desk, I was stunned to see that my hands were shaking. I never like to admit it when things are tough for me to handle, but I guess everything had just all built up a little too much. I looked out the window and saw that the women were gone. I was really glad that was over with.

Or so I thought.

About an hour later, from his perch two hundred feet above the scene, my tower crane operator called me on the phone. "Hey, Barry!" he said. "I just saw—the cops are at Edith's house!"

By the time I hightailed it over there, the cops were already through her gate. They hadn't knocked on her door before I said, "Hello, officers, can I help you?"

"We just got a report that a lady is being held against her will in this house," one of the officers said.

One of those women must have called the cops. Damn, some people can be persistent. And annoying.

"Well, that's not the case, officer," I said.

"We're going to have to see her," he replied.

I knocked on the door, then stuck my head in, and said, "Edith, it's Barry. The police are here. They want to know if you're okay."

"I'm fine!" she yelled from the couch. "Tell them to get the hell out of here!"

"They're going to have to come in, Edith."

"Tell them to go to hell! I'm a U.S. citizen! I have my rights!"

The cops looked at each other, and kind of smiled. They thanked me for my trouble, and headed on their way.

It was just a little bit after that that I decided to give in and talk to some of the media folks who'd been pestering me. I figured, maybe people couldn't make up their own stories if I gave them the truth.

Some of them just never got it right. There was this one reporter who came over to the construction trailer and wanted to interview me. I said I was in a meeting right at that moment, but that she could come by at 3:00; she didn't show up, but on the news that night, she reported the latest "update" on the Edith story, whatever it was, and said that I refused to comment. And *The Seattle Times* seemed to always have it in for me. I don't know what it was about those guys.

But I will say that the rest of them, the TV stations, once I started sitting down and giving them interviews, they got it right. I just told them the truth. The developers had offered her the money and she turned it down, and now I'm in there taking care of her because she wants to die in that house and I'm going to do whatever I can to make sure she gets what she wants.

It seemed to do the trick. The media storm calmed down. But it was really just a distraction, in the end. I was still feeling pretty overwhelmed with all that taking care of Edith was taking out of me, and it didn't seem like there was anywhere I could turn to get away. But I did need to get away, so I planned a deer-hunting trip with my brother-in-law that October. It didn't come up very much, but whenever I was going away, I'd warn Edith a week, two weeks ahead of time, just to get her warmed up to the idea. Then as the weekend approached I'd remind her. I'd reassure her that everything was going to be okay, and I'd show her where I'd left the phone numbers of the people who said they'd come by if she needed them.

Saturday morning came, and I was up in the early, early morning, a steaming cup of coffee in the holder next to me in the truck, the damp night air seeping in around the truck windows, some AC/DC music on the CD player. My shoulders, which had been hunched up around my ears for about a month, finally started to drop a little. I had left about four a.m., so that we could be out before daylight. I turned onto the highway toward my brother-in-law's place in Chehalis, about two and a half hours away, and I had gotten maybe thirty miles down the road, down to about Renton, when my cell phone rang.

Edith.

No, I thought. You are not going to ruin this one for me.

"I'm on the floor," she said, "and I made a mess."

I looked at the highway stretching out in front of me, my headlights eating up the dotted white lines. I thought of the smell of the woods in the morning, the feeling of being out with some jerky and a thermos, sitting in the quiet, waiting for the sound of a hoof breaking a branch.

It was a nice dream.

I let out a long, deep breath. "I'll be right there," I said, and headed back to Edith's, to clean up one more mess.

As I drove back, I started thinking about how differently I would have been handling this moment if it had been my dad that had called instead of Edith. I hadn't talked to my dad in a while, but I realized how very impatient I had been getting with him. His forgetfulness, his crankiness, his attitude in general were just bothering me, and I wasn't having any problem letting him know it. Each time he'd call me by my brother's name or call my brother by mine, or get angry at my mother for something ridiculous like one of his socks being inside out or something, I'd get a little more upset. I guess it was no secret that I was getting annoyed.

And yet for the most part I was staying pretty patient with Edith, even though she sure wasn't making it easy for me. What is it that makes us more tolerant of all sorts of behavior in other people and so intolerant of it in our relatives—the ones we love the most and probably owe the most to? I don't know the answer to that, and I figured that I didn't really need to. The point is simply *that* we do it, not *why* we do it.

My philosophy's a pretty simple one: You figure out what the right thing to do is, and you try to do that thing. It doesn't really matter why you weren't doing it up until now. I don't need to go sit on a psychiatrist's couch to figure this one out. The point is just that Edith needed me now, and if I didn't help her out, then no one was going to do it and she'd be up a creek. And while my dad didn't need my care right now, he did need my patience, and I at least owed him that.

The sun was still not up when I pulled in front of Edith's house, but the sky was not quite as dark as it had been. Through her window I noticed the yellow light coming from the lamp near the door, so I knew she'd at least tried to get up before she'd fallen. It was a clammy and cold morning, but after I turned the key in the lock and pushed the door open, I felt a waft of warm air from inside.

It was such a sad sight, Edith in the middle of the floor in the middle of a big mess. I felt so sorry for her. I don't know what I was expecting her to say, but I wasn't at all surprised by her welcome:

"Well, what the hell took you so long?"

After a while, when I'd managed to get everything cleaned up, I looked out the window. The damp air of the morning was seeping in now, and the sky had turned the color of an old forgotten battleship. It was still early enough for me to try to salvage what was left of my day of deer hunting. I called Evie and asked her to look in on Edith, and headed back to my truck.

We actually did manage to get a deer that day; we'd finished gutting it and were hauling it back to the truck when I felt my cell phone vibrate. It was Evie, calling to tell me that she and my daughter had checked in on Edith, and sure enough she'd fallen again and left another big mess. Evie didn't seem the least bit upset about it—in fact, from the sound of things in the background, you'd think they were having a gay old party. Evie told me not to worry, to take my time and relax, and that she had my back for the afternoon.

God bless Evie.

It wasn't long after that that I started going down to Edith's on the weekends as well. I talked to Evie about it, and we agreed that the difficulty of trying to cover things when I was away was more hassle than just driving down and doing what I had to do. Soon I was at Edith's seven days a week, every week. Evie and Kelsey would come down some weekends and help clean up the house. I loved that Kelsey was so quick to bond with Edith. We never made her come; she always wanted to. When I heard Kelsey and Edith and Evie chatting away, it did my heart a lot of good. Kelsey wouldn't take any money from Edith for cleaning, but Edith would insist. "A college girl needs money, my dear," she would say.

Willy wasn't as enthusiastic, but he did his part without complaining. There was a big wooden fence around three sides of Edith's property, and the taggers had hit it pretty good. Edith got a notice from the city that if she didn't clean up the graffiti they would, and they'd charge her for it; so one day Willy and I mixed up all the paint we could find in my garage and poured it into a bucket. It came out a kind of dark gray. I drove Willy down with me and gave him a five-minute lesson on what I needed done, and left it to him while I went to the trailer to get some work done. I checked on him once in a while, but didn't really need to. He did a fine job painting that fence.

But the days that Evie and Kelsey came down to help clean, or Willy came down to do one chore or another, were about the only times I'd see them, and I was feeling pretty lousy about that. After I'd been at Edith's a few Saturdays I began to wonder, had I created a monster? Edith wasn't the healthiest person in the world, but she was a tough little cookie. This wasn't hospice care I was doing. It's not like I was holding her hand as she quietly let go and slipped over to the other side. This was a feisty old woman who seemed to have every intention of hanging on for a long time, and making my life as difficult as possible in the process.

That's a terribly, terribly guilty thought for anyone taking care of an old person. You want with all your heart to keep them alive as long as you can. You try to ignore the little selfish person inside you that is terrified of just how long that could be. What if she lives to be a hundred? You think. What am I going to do when the mall job is finished? What if I'm taking care of Edith long after my kids are grown and married? Exactly how much am I willing to give up? And then you feel so incredibly guilty for even thinking that, that you try to turn your mind to other things. Fortunately for me, I was always pretty good at that.

Also fortunately for me, Edith was pretty good at distracting me as well. She always had something up her sleeve.

Anyone who commutes to work five days a week knows how much you don't want to make that commute on the weekends, let alone twice on the weekends, so some Saturday nights I slept on the floor. But as often as I could, I was still driving home on the weekends, just to keep as much of a semblance of a normal family life as possible.

I didn't catch on at first, but Edith was setting her alarm to watch the early news shows on Sundays, so that by the time I got there and we started watching *Meet the Press*, she'd be way ahead of me. We had some lively conversations on those mornings—you don't expect someone that old to be so progressive, or to think that new is better than old; but she was just disgusted with what she called the "old thinking" of guys like John McCain and, to some degree, even Hillary Clinton.

It reminded me of her conversation about the Kingdome—how they'd torn it down just twenty-five years after they built it, and how she knew they'll tear down the mall, too, one day. We had talked about that such a long time ago, but it stayed with me. I remember wondering then how this old woman could be so accepting of change on the one hand, and so insanely stubborn on the other. After more than a year of talking to her, of hearing her stories and dealing with her day-to-day life, I didn't feel any closer to an answer. Maybe it had something to do with all the pain and loss she'd suffered; maybe part of her wanted to cling to what was past, and part of her wanted to forget all about it and just move on.

One Sunday morning, as we were watching the news shows, I happened to notice those four etchings on the wall of the living room that I'd admired a bunch of times, tarnished square plaques halfway between silver and gold, about half the size of a piece of printer paper, in old, cracked black frames. Two were of a courtyard in what looked like an Italian city, and the others were sailboats at a waterfront. The sun broke through the clouds while we were watching *Meet the Press*, and glinted off one of those etchings.

"Edith, are those supposed to be Venice?" I asked. I didn't know much about Italy, but I know a canal when I see one.

It took her a moment to move from the current events on the TV to the distant memory of those etchings. "Yes, Venice, of course," she said. "Lionel Barrymore did those. He gave them to me."

"Lionel Barrymore," I said, not really as a question, more like a challenge. I don't know why I still doubted her as much as I did—the sheer number of these stories seemed to give them some truth, just from the collective weight of them—but each time another one showed up it was like starting over for me. Outside of the fact that she did actually seem to be Benny Goodman's cousin, I still didn't have a shred of hard evidence of any of it: teaching Mickey Rooney to dance, buying Tommy Dorsey's saxophone, marrying Richard Tauber, anything. So when a brand-new claim would appear like a woodchuck from a burrow, I'd feel the reflex to take a shot at it.

As the pundits on the TV were going on about George Bush and Iraq, I pulled the story out of her, bit by bit. She said she was working with "some movie people"—I couldn't get her to be more specific than that—and one Sunday morning they needed her to take a script over to Lionel Barrymore.

He invited her in, and they chatted for a while. She tried to ask him about himself, she said, but he only wanted to talk about her. In fact, he told her that the next time she came, which he hoped would be soon, he would have a present for her. And sure enough, the next time she ran an errand to his house, he gave her two of the etchings. A little while later he gave her two more.

It was the one with the sailboat that always caught my eye, and the sun was reflecting off of it now as she told the story. Edith turned her attention back to the TV, and I walked over to take a closer look at the etching. I have no idea how those are done, but you could see if you looked at the right angle that someone had actually carved the picture into the metal.

I never noticed it before, but something else was carved into the metal as well.

In print that was tiny but still quite legible, at the bottom right corner, it read, "L. Barrymore."

I looked over at Edith. She was shaking her head.

"They're all a bunch of idiots," she said, referring to the TV. "All a bunch of goddamn good-for-nothing useless idiots."

10

People ask me if I felt guilty about spending so much time with Edith, after my dad was diagnosed with Alzheimer's. I really didn't. For one, I knew he could still take care of himself, and he had my mom there. Edith needed me a lot more. For another, I know that he and my mom were really proud of me for what I was doing. Especially my mom, since she'd done it herself so many times. It was a stand-up thing to do, they told me, and I guess you never get too old to feel pleased when your parents tell you you're a good boy.

I was only seeing my dad every couple of months, but I was talking to him a lot more often now. I just felt the need to. I had talked to Dad after the doctor told him that he couldn't drive anymore. That was hard for him to take. He went along with the idea—he understood and all—but it was really kind of sad because he was always one for wanting to go for a drive.

When we were kids, you always knew when we were

headed somewhere, because he'd pace around the house, acting all antsy, and jingling the car keys in his pocket. And you
just knew he was figuring out where we were going to go. It's
not that he wanted to go anyplace in particular, he just didn't
want to be right where he was anymore. And then all of a sudden, he'd say, "Pack up, we're going," and we'd all bolt for the
car. We didn't ask him where we were going, because we
knew he wouldn't tell us; looking back, I bet half the time he
didn't know where we were going himself. Sometimes he'd
take the most circuitous route to get someplace, whether it
was some friend's house or down to the doughnut shop, and
you didn't know if he was trying to throw you off the scent,
or if he just hadn't settled on his destination until after he'd
backed out of the driveway. That was just a force in his life,
and none of us gave it a second thought. It was who he was,
and you accepted it, and took a kind of secret delight in it.

But now, as we grappled with the Alzheimer's and all that
went with it, so much had changed. One morning my mother
was sleeping upstairs and he was sleeping on the couch. Even
before the Alzheimer's, he had been suffering from some
pretty bad migraines, and had started huddling up alone on
the couch, with a blanket over his head so the light couldn't get
in; it was about the only way either of them could get any
sleep. When he quit working, the migraines went away, but he
had gotten into the habit of falling asleep on the couch, watching TV, and a lot of times he'd just stay there for the night.

When my mom woke up that morning and didn't see hide
nor hair of him, she just assumed he was sleeping down on
the couch. But he wasn't. He was gone, and so was the truck.

Mom realized then that she'd heard him go out a little earlier, but she'd thought he was just going out to get the paper, and didn't think any more of it. She figured that had to have been about six o'clock. Now it was 9:30. So wherever the heck he was, he had a pretty good head start.

Mom was panicking pretty badly. Her concern was compounded by the fear that since Dad wasn't supposed to be driving, we would be liable for anything that happened in case of an accident. She called my brother and a little while later she called me.

"He's making me crazy," she said. "He's just making me crazy. I don't know how much more of this I can take."

I wanted to reassure her. I wanted to help her. But there wasn't much I could do. Dad didn't have a cell phone, and it's not like we were about to put out an APB on the guy. I tried to reassure my mom that he was going to be fine, that he'd been driving since 1950 and could probably handle a little joyride even now. And the truth was, I wasn't too worried. Even with the Alzheimer's, Dad was still sharp as a tack a lot of the time. When he got tired, though, he seemed to get worse, so as the day wore on and no one heard from him, I started to get more concerned.

It didn't help that we had a history of this in the family. Years ago, my dad's mom was diagnosed with Alzheimer's. She had been living with my aunt when one day she just up and left. They found her on a bus at the Greyhound station in Spokane. We never figured out what the hell was in Spokane. She just got it into her head that she was going, and there she went. So underlying all of this was the fear that Dad had just got it into his head to go somewhere, and now he was gone, who knows where. I offered to call the cops in Spokane, but no one thought that was very funny.

We kept hoping he was coming to visit one of us, my brother or my sister or me. We spent the day all frantically calling each other—"Any sign of him?" "Any word?"—as though he might show up and we'd forget to let everyone else know. Then, just when we really were getting ready to actually put out the APB, he comes waltzing in the front door, calm as can be, as though he *had* just gone out to get the paper.

Turns out that Dad had gone to visit his cousin up in Ravensdale, about an hour and a half away. My mom actually slapped her forehead, like you see in the movies, because he'd given her lots of hints of this, but she just never put two and two together. For the last few weeks, she said, he'd been talking to her about going to visit a cousin he hadn't seen for a long time. Mom kept putting it off, because they didn't even know this cousin's phone number, didn't even know if she was still living in Ravensdale. Mom wasn't really up for a wild-goose chase, so when he brought it up she kept changing the subject. It never occurred to her that he would just decide to up and go by himself.

Dad filled my mom in on the whole thing, as calmly as could be. He had caught the car ferry and got off in Edmonds, to see my brother. When he wasn't there, he headed out to Ravensdale, way out in the boonstickers, looking for his cousin's house. And wouldn't you know it, he actually found her. They visited for a while, and then Dad came back home. So what's the big deal? he wondered.

Well, at that, Mom told me, she had gotten furious, and started reading him the riot act. "You're not even supposed to be driving!" she said. "Let alone driving all the way out to Ravensdale! Let alone not even telling anyone where you were! What were you thinking? What were you *thinking*?"

The funny thing was that Dad stayed pretty calm through it all. I think before he got Alzheimer's, he was more likely to fly off the handle and get really upset—at himself or everyone else. But as I said, it was almost like the Alzheimer's gave him an explanation that he could live with, and that kept him calm.

The other funny thing was that I stayed calm through it all.

I went to see him the next day. My mom and my brother were still worked up into a pretty good lather. But when Dad and I sat down together in the living room with a couple of sodas, it was about the most—I guess you'd say sane—conversation we'd had in years. If this had happened a year earlier, I would have been furious at him. Now it was different.

"You know you have Alzheimer's and you really shouldn't do this," I said. "We're just afraid you're going to get lost. I know you always had a pretty good sense of direction, but you can't count on that anymore. You gotta know that."

"I hear ya," Dad said. "It was nice to get out for a bit, though." He smiled, just a little bit. Despite myself, I guess I did, too. I think Dad was accepting what I was saying because I wasn't judging him. I wasn't condemning him. I understood that even though he had a disease, he was still in charge of his own life. I respected that, which made it easier for all of us. I was acting like it was his decision whether or not to try this stunt again, and by the end of the conversation he promised that he wouldn't.

As I left that afternoon, and I thought about how differently I would have handled this just a little while earlier, I said, out loud, but quietly so no one would hear:

"Thanks, Edith."

As I drove home, I thought about a conversation I'd had with my brother on the phone earlier that day. "Wait till I get hold of him," my brother had said. "I'm going to give him a good talking to, you can count on that." That's just what I would have said, I think, if I hadn't learned what I'd learned from my dealings with Edith. It's why I had wangled it that I would talk to him first. Because I knew now that you just can't do that. You can't spank your father.

I mean, sure, he could have gotten lost. But it's not like the Alzheimer's made him forget which side of the road to drive on or which pedal is the brake. We had a frightening day; but he had a great one. Helping him understand why he shouldn't do that—for his own good—is very different from punishing him for being a bad boy.

That's the distinction that Edith taught me. I'm really glad she did.

Edith fell down a number of times that winter. Too often, I'd come over and find her on the floor. But she still wouldn't let me bring in any help, and in fact was getting even more demanding of my time. It seemed like every time I tried to leave she manufactured some kind of crisis. It all came to a head one morning, after I'd made her sloppy toast and was getting ready to head over to the construction trailer.

"Wait," she gasped. "I can't breathe. I can't breathe!"

Oh, this again, I thought. It was way too convenient—and way too theatrical—for me to take seriously, so I made another joke about where she took her acting lessons. I know there was no need for that, but I was feeling a little pissed off that morning. And it's tough to deal with someone who's getting old and sick and ornery, especially if they had a big head start on the ornery part. I was learning to make adjustments for Edith. Maybe I had to make some adjustments for myself, too. You have to allow yourself to let off a little steam once in a while, and I guess this was my morning for that.

"I can't breathe!" she insisted. I'll admit that the first time I saw this routine I was pretty freaked out, but by now I was immune to it. And impatient, to boot. I wasn't going to be late for the morning meeting because Edith had decided it was time to put on a show.

"You're fine, Edith," I said, as calmly and compassionately as I could, given the fact that I wasn't feeling particularly calm or compassionate right at that moment. "You're fine. Just relax."

"I need the ambulance!" she gasped. "Call them!"

"You need them, you call them," I said. And with that I walked out the door.

I stopped about ten times on the way to the trailer, wondering if I was being too harsh. I mean, an old lady is gasping for the ambulance and you don't dial 911? That doesn't exactly rank very high in the responsibility book. But I was feeling the weight of the last few months on my shoulders, and I felt like just this once, I had to shrug it off or I'd collapse. This is a marathon, I kept telling myself, not a sprint. You can't spend all your energy at every moment.

I forced myself to keep walking to the trailer, and about ten minutes later, one of the guys yelled from outside the window, "Hey, Barry, aid car's here!" And I just yelled out, "Thanks," and let it go.

After a few minutes, my curiosity got the better of me, so I wandered back over.

We had called the aid car a number of times over the last few months, so the EMTs knew me pretty well by now. They greeted me by name and asked after Evie, and didn't seem overly concerned. They asked me when she fell and got the latest crop of bruises, and when I told them it was more than a week ago they looked at Edith like they'd just caught her in a lie. No one said anything, though. They told me they'd gone through the whole routine of checking her blood oxygen level, which was fine, and I made another remark about her being a good actress, and Edith made another remark about wanting to go to the hospital, and suddenly everyone in the room was looking at me, as if I was the chess master about to announce the next move.

Not much to think about, really. "She wants to go, take her," I said. "See you later, Edith," and I walked out again. This time I didn't have any second thoughts.

They put her through a whole battery of tests that day, X-rays and a CT scan and a full blood workup. At about four that afternoon I got a call. "This is the ER," they said. "She's ready to come home. When do you want to come get her?" It seemed like everyone knew our routine by now.

"I'm not coming," I told them. There was silence on the other end of the line. "You took her, you bring her back."

It was about an hour before the aid car showed up again. When they brought Edith out in a wheelchair, she was out like she was comatose. I walked up, and the aid guy—a different one than the one from that morning—asked, "Are you Barry?" I said, and he said, "Yeah, before she went out she was yellin' for ya."

I started wheeling her into the house, and she came around (or stopped pretending to be asleep, more likely), and immediately started cursing a blue streak. "This fucking idiot couldn't find the house," she said. "We've been driving around for an hour. Where the hell were you?"

She didn't curse like that too often, but often enough. It still shocked the hell out of me to hear those words coming from someone like her. "Glad you're okay, Edith" was all I said, and I got her into the house and onto the couch, and started cooking her dinner.

We didn't say another word about the whole incident, but something changed after that. It seemed like once again we'd forged a new understanding: I'm here to help you, and I'll do everything I can to help you, but if you start yanking my chain I'm going to call you on it.

I didn't get any more of those I-can't-breathe incidents after that, and I thought, well, I guess I've got this monster under control.

That's one of those lies you tell yourself for as long as you can, until reality comes around and slaps you one and says, guess again, smart boy.

You know those goofy commercials you see on TV for the electric wheelchair that can go around corners, pull a two-ton van, and get two old ladies to the Grand Canyon, and all that? Well, a few months earlier, I'd tried to get Edith to use one of those things. It's called a Hoveround. It's not a wheelchair, exactly; more like a motor scooter, kind of like a car seat on wheels. She was having a hard time with the walker, and I thought this would be easier for her. She could just jump on this hush puppy and get around the house, go down the block, whatever.

Edith was not exactly thrilled.

"I don't know why you brought that thing," she said. "I'm not going to use it. What a pain. Who needs it?"

I left it there for about two weeks, thinking she'd eventually give in. Why I thought her stubborn streak would suddenly vanish, I don't know. She did ride it once—to move it out of the way. She drove it into a corner near the stairs, and there it sat until I finally took it away. I realized after the fact that it was another case of doing what would make things easier for me, something to make me feel a little less guilty when I couldn't be there. It wasn't what Edith needed. It certainly wasn't what she wanted.

Funny, the number of times I had to keep learning that lesson.

So the second time I brought up the subject, I was a little more delicate, and she was a little more willing to discuss it. This time, I asked her if she'd consider my getting her an old-fashioned wheelchair, and she was sort of amenable to the idea. She did have a big old one that was pretty useless, since it was too wide to use in the house, and too bulky and heavy to take anywhere without a lot of hassle. She finally agreed to let me get a decent wheelchair. Now, when we'd go to the doctor's office or something, it would be a lot easier for the both of us. Easier for her, being the main point. She still wasn't using it around the house too much—which, secretly, is the reason I wanted her to get the smaller one. She hadn't taken to the idea. She was still trying to use the walker indoors. Not with all that much success, I might add.

One night she called me at home—it must have been near midnight—and told me she'd fallen and had an accident on the floor again. Evie was really starting to get kind of irritated about these late-night calls, but I still got a thermos of hot chocolate and a kiss good-bye as I headed out the door.

The moon was bright and a light snow was falling, and it was actually kind of peaceful heading down the road, which was in great contrast to the mess I saw when I walked through Edith's door. By the time I'd gotten her into the bathtub, and cleaned the rug and changed all the bedding, it was way too late for me to drive home, so I just made up a corner of the floor and went to sleep in about two minutes.

I have no idea what time it was when I heard a "thunk, thunk, thunk" in the night. I looked up, and there was Edith, using that big old commode as a walker. I asked her what the hell she was doing, and she said she was cold, so she was going over to turn the heat up.

"Why didn't you just wake me up?" I asked her, sounding a little more annoyed than I meant to.

"Oh, you know," she said, in the most innocent voice you can imagine, "I don't like to trouble you."

I just had to smile at that one. But on a certain level, that was very real, for her. As much of a pain in the butt as she could be, she really didn't want to be beholden to anyone. Like when she'd start worrying about her medical bills and I suggested that she take out a reverse mortgage on her house, she wouldn't even consider it, because she didn't want to owe anyone anything.

Which is not to say that she went out of her way to make anything easier for me.

As I said, after the whole incident with the aid car, I thought we'd come to a kind of tacit understanding of what the limits were. I guess in a sense we had, although my definition of those limits and hers clearly weren't one and the same.

It hadn't been that long ago that she was eating nothing more than Stouffer's frozen dinners, so I was still a little sensitive about trying to get some better food into her. She had been losing weight lately, and the more I tried to fatten her up, the more she seemed to be slipping in the other direction. But I kept trying. I don't like to brag, but I'd been fixing Edith some fairly decent dinners; I wouldn't call them gourmet dining, but I wouldn't argue with someone if they did. It was real food, well prepared; healthy and tasty, too.

A few days after that latest late-night fiasco, I finished up at work a little early and decided I'd make Edith a nice meal, then go home and make a meal for Evie and me as well. I picked up some fresh fish and vegetables at the market, and put mine in Edith's fridge while I was preparing her dinner. I poached some halibut, and made some sugar snap peas and baby red potatoes, the whole ball of wax.

I brought it in and set it out on the table, along with everything she'd need for the night. When she noticed me doing that, she got her hackles up. "Where the hell are you going?" she snapped.

I don't know why I expected anything different; they say insanity is doing the same thing over and over and expecting a different outcome, so I guess you could chalk me up as insane right at that moment.

I told her I was going to go home early and have dinner with my wife, and something in my tone must have incensed her, because she started cursing something awful. "Fine!" she yelled. "Just leave me here alone to die, why don't you! I knew you couldn't stick it out! Go!"

I guess I didn't look hurt enough by that, so for good measure, she grabbed the edge of the coffee table, with her lovely dinner and a glass of milk on it, and yanked it up as high as she could and let go. The food went flying first, followed by the plate. The table seemed to lag a few beats behind, but finally came crashing down with the rest of it. Just to give more drama to the moment, she reached out with her foot and gave the table a swift kick.

That did it.

I looked around to grab whatever I could find. The closest

thing to me was a box of baby wipes that we kept next to the commode. I reached for it and drop-kicked it across the room, and gave the plate and the halibut on the floor a swift kick as well. "That's the way you want it, fine," I said. "I'm outta here." I grabbed my food from the refrigerator and stormed toward the door, with Edith's screams raining down on me. "I knew you couldn't stick it out!" she yelled again.

"I'm not quitting," I said, and I could feel the veins popping out of my neck as I was talking. "I don't go back on my word and you can't make me. I will see you in the morning." I slammed the door behind me, gunned the motor, squealed my tires a little as I pulled away from the curb, and headed for home.

I probably got about four miles down the road before my cell phone rang. The voice that came through the phone sounded like that of a frightened child.

"You didn't leave me enough water," Edith said. "I hate to bother you, but can you come bring me some water? I just don't feel I can do it myself."

I let out a long sigh. Again I thought, this is a marathon, not a sprint.

"I'll be right there," I said, and pressed the red button on my cell, and pulled off at the next exit, and swung around back toward Edith's again.

I got back, and we didn't talk much. The TV was on, as always, and I just cleaned up the mess. When I was done I asked her if she was hungry, and she said she was, so I looked in the fridge, and told her what we had for frozen dinners, and that was about that.

But as I was leaving, finally, to get home, and paused to make sure there was enough water on the table, she reached out and touched my arm.

"You don't know," she said, "in the night, how I long to hear your key in the door. Sometimes I lie awake for hours, waiting for the morning, waiting for the sound of your key in the door."

Well, you could have knocked me over with a feather at that point. It was probably the first time, through all of this, that she'd gotten so close to a thank-you. I wasn't in it for the gratitude, of course, but it was still pretty damn nice to hear. I couldn't believe I was hearing it.

I couldn't believe what came out of my mouth either, at that point. I leaned over, and I kissed her on the forehead, and I said, "I love you, old woman. Now get some sleep."

11

The snows came harder than usual that year, the winter of 2007, but the roads were clear on the way to my dad's house. I hadn't wanted to leave Edith alone, but she said she didn't mind, that she hadn't celebrated Christmas in years. So we all piled into the car and got an early start.

I like to think of Christmas as controlled chaos. My brother and sister were there: Malinda came with her two boys, who were now pushing thirty; Jeffery, the younger of the two, had three kids under the age of six, so that added to the fun. My kids were growing up fast. Kelsey was eighteen and Willy was seventeen that Christmas. My brother Randy's two kids were younger; he had a nine- and a five-year-old. So we had just about every age range, crowded into that one living room, and it seemed like everybody was talking at once.

We decided to have the holiday at my folks' house, because my dad was getting kind of jittery when there was too much chaos around. Distracted, too. We'd seen it pretty often, when he'd come to visit. Before you knew it, he was pacing around, jingling the change in his pocket the way he used to jingle the car keys, wanting to leave. So we figured, if we had it at his place he couldn't go anywhere.

He still seemed a little nervous with all of us there. He took the dog out for a walk a couple of times, and went upstairs once or twice to be by himself. Other than that, there wasn't much indication of anything wrong with him. Or maybe that was wishful thinking. Dad's mobility was waning, and he was pretty winded when he came in from walking the dog. He lost his train of thought in the middle of a conversation more than once that day, and got a little frustrated when he couldn't think of a word, but the anger that we'd seen the previous year was pretty much gone. I think in the days before we knew the word *Alzheimer's* we would have just chalked all this up to Grandpa being Grandpa. After the diagnosis, we all watched for signs of decline more carefully. Probably a little too carefully, and I guess that didn't help much.

At one point, when he was upstairs, I wandered into the kitchen and asked my mom how they were doing. As I said, they're from a generation that didn't open up much, kept a lot inside, so I was surprised to hear how honest she was about it all.

"I can't do a lot of the things I used to do," she said, stirring some cranberry sauce on the stove. "I don't go out to play bridge or anything like that. I can't leave him alone for four hours. I don't know if he's going to leave the stove on, or go out for a walk and get lost."

It took a lot for her to admit that. But there wasn't a hint of resentment in her voice. She sounded a little scared, I guess. Scared of what might come, or of all the responsibility she had. None of us lived closer than an hour away, so it wasn't like we could pop by while she was at the grocery store; but when I asked her about that, again, she didn't give a hint of feeling sorry for herself. I guess that's part of what made up folks in her generation too.

The next day, I went to Edith's. I didn't bring her a present, because she had made it clear that she didn't want to have anything to do with Christmas. I wondered if there was any point in asking why, but I couldn't help myself; I just had to ask anyway. And to my surprise, I got an answer.

"Because of one of my stepchildren," she said. Apparently that's how she referred to the children at the orphanage she ran in England, the one she started after she talked to the rich man at a party long, long ago. She said she had "adopted" them and considered all of them her stepchildren.

"There was a house down the hill from the orphanage," she told me. "It was Christmas, and all the children were gathered at the orphanage, except for one of the older children. He was in the army, and he was staying at that house with his wife. And I wondered why he hadn't come up for the party, so I went down to see after him."

Edith was propped up on the side of the couch, clutching a light blue sweater around her. She pulled it a little tighter, as if to fend off a sudden chill.

She didn't look at me as she described the scene she found at that house. She had knocked and called and no one had

answered, she said. But the heavy wooden door was un-
locked, so she let herself in, and walked through the narrow
room to the bedroom in the back.

There she saw her stepson's wife, and next to her a strange
man Edith had never seen before. Both of them were nude,
their lifeless bodies bloody and limp.

Edith said she didn't notice right away, but when she looked
around, she saw her stepson, slumped on the floor next to the
bed, a gun at his side.

"He found his wife in bed with another man," Edith told
me. There was no emotion in her voice. "Apparently he shot
them both, then blew his brains out. Blew his brains out," she
repeated, as though she was trying to convince herself it was
true.

"After that I had to go back to the house and pretend nothing had happened. I didn't want to ruin Christmas for the
other children. They had so little in their lives. I couldn't take
that away from them. But since then, that's it for me. I don't
want a tree. I don't want a card. I don't want a present."

I didn't know what to say. Surely she couldn't be making
this up. I couldn't even get my mind around it—something
so brutal, so terrible. And on Christmas, of all things. No one,
I don't care who they are, could make up a story like that. Yet
how could this possibly have happened? How can you know
somebody for almost two years and see them every day and
they never mention a word of it?

Edith didn't seem to be waiting for any kind of reaction.
She had turned back to the television. Judge Judy was giving

somebody a hard time about something. I couldn't really focus on it.

I did a little mental math and figured that those orphans were probably in their mid-sixties by now.

"Edith," I finally said, "what happened to all those children? Do you ever see any of them?"

She didn't turn away from the TV. "No, that's the past," she said, as though that was enough of an answer.

"But what happened to all of them?" I asked again.

"When I left them to come to America to take care of my mother, they were very upset," she told me. "They begged me not to go. Begged and begged. I tried to explain that I had to take care of my mother, that I was all she had. They said 'But you're all we have.' And that was true, I guess. I knew what they were saying. But still, I had to go, and they couldn't understand. In the end, they said they would never speak to me again if I left. It's understandable, after all they'd been through. But I had to do what I had to do. So I never heard from them again. Well, you make your bed, you lie in it," she said, and that was that.

She started flipping around the channels with the remote.

"Whatever happened to that castle in Cornwall?" I asked.

"I made a lot of money from the sheep I raised there," she said, not really answering the question. She had opened the buttons on the blue sweater and was fiddling with it now, pulling it back so it hung a little more loosely. "The fellow who owned the castle told me I couldn't take any of the money with me to the States. I guess that was fair. But you see, when your people offer me a million dollars, they don't know that I've had it once and walked away from it. Money isn't everything, Barry. It isn't even close."

I knew better than to ask any more questions. This was probably the longest conversation we'd ever had about her past. I didn't have the slightest idea how to find out if what she was telling me had really happened. When I talked to Evie about it that night, she was as amazed, and confused, as I was. Two thoughts kept coming up, two opposing thoughts, one as strong as the other:

How could this story possibly be true?

How could it possibly not?

12

When winter digs its heels in good and steady, the people of Seattle can get a little cranky. It's cold and gray, and the days don't seem to be in any hurry to get any longer. In lots of places, people make the joke "If you don't like the weather here, just wait a minute, and it'll change." In Seattle, the joke goes, "That's right—it'll stop raining, and start pouring." After a while, the gloom really wears people down pretty good.

Edith seemed a little more off her feed than usual, as well, although it took a while for me to realize that it was something other than the weather. Something seemed to be going on with her that I couldn't put my finger on. She was peeing a lot more lately—a whole lot more—and it seemed like no matter how much food I was pumping into her she couldn't keep her weight up. Her ornery side kept me from taking her to the hospital for tests, and I couldn't force her. Or I wouldn't try, I should say.

Again, I had learned to keep a balance between doing

what I thought was best for her, and giving her enough say in the day-to-day decisions about her life that she could maintain her dignity and respect.

She did, finally, agree to go for the tests. I got to work extra early that day to get everything done, because I had a feeling the day was going to be a long one. It sure started out with all the signs of that.

"Morning, Edith. How are you doing this morning?"

"If they paid a person to pee I'd be a rich woman."

"I brought you some socks."

"I don't want 'em. Leave me alone."

"Aren't your feet cold?"

"If my feet were cold I'd put socks on, wouldn't I."

It was one of those conversations that I knew would have gone a whole lot differently a year earlier. I felt the need to convince her to put her socks on, to take charge the way you would with your kids. But I had come to understand that the chance of her dying from cold feet was pretty slim, but the chance of her blowing her top because someone was trying to tell her whether to put on socks was pretty high. I put the socks on the stairs going up, and asked her if she was ready to get the show on the road.

"Why the hell are we going to the doctors," she said, not as a question as much as a challenge.

"You agreed," I reminded her. It had been a rough couple of weeks. No matter what I fed her, she lost more weight. I bought some cans of Ensure, which was supposed to give her all the nutrition she needed. And I felt like between the Ensure, and all the fatty foods I could get her to eat, and the gallons of water she was drinking every day, that the whole day was about Incoming and Outgoing. The more I pumped into her, the more she was on that commode. She was complaining that her butt was sore from sitting on the thing so often.

But even through all that, I was having a terrible time convincing her to go to the doctor's. She didn't like the hospital in Ballard, so I had made appointments for her to go to the big Harborview Medical Center down in the First Hill area just outside Seattle—Pill Hill, everybody calls it. When we did start driving, she kept squirming and fussing around in her seat, like a child on the way to school who's afraid there's going to be a pop quiz. Sure enough, as we turned off the interstate just a few blocks from the hospital, she announced, "I'm not going. Take me home. I'm not going."

I let out a sigh.

"Edith, we talked about this," I said, halfheartedly, knowing how unlikely it was that I was going to get her to budge.

"And when we talked about it I said I didn't want to go, and I meant it. Now turn this vehicle around, please."

I argued with her for a few more minutes, but I knew it was no use. I guess there was a part of me that knew it wasn't my place to push her. She didn't trust doctors, so pretty often when they would tell her something—to go on a new drug, or whatever—she'd say no, I'm not doing it. But I'd take in the information, and at a calmer moment I'd go through it with her. Sometimes I could convince her. Sometimes I couldn't. But I also knew that I had to make sure it was for her own good, not for mine, that I was talking her into stuff. This certainly was a borderline case: Did I want her to take the tests today because I knew she needed them, or because I'd driven all the way down here and didn't want to waste my time?

Fair question. I didn't really have to answer it, though, because she wasn't changing her mind either way.

I had to take a couple of right turns to find my way back to the highway, and they happened to take us right past the entrance to the hospital. It was a big, imposing building—two buildings, really, across the street from each other, identical in architecture but one about three times taller than the other. As we headed past them toward the highway, I asked one more time, "Are you sure you don't want to just go in as long as we're here?"

"I'm sure I don't want to go in as long as we're here," Edith replied. And that was about that.

In the weeks that followed, I regretted that I hadn't pushed harder for her to go to the hospital. Things were getting worse. Edith seemed more fragile every day. And it wasn't just her health. She couldn't get around very much at all on her own. That was bad enough, but when she finally had to admit that she couldn't write at all anymore, she got really upset. I realized that I still didn't know exactly what she was working on, and felt embarrassed that I hadn't asked. Maybe it was another novel or something. Whatever it was, I knew it was important to her and boosted her spirits, so one after-noon I asked her if I could bring Kelsey over and Edith could dictate whatever she was working on. Edith very politely said thanks, but that wasn't at all how she worked, and it would never do. I looked over at that big doorstop of a book on her desk, *Where Yesterday Began*, by Domilini—Edith's pen name—

and felt a wave of sadness. Now that Edith couldn't write, it was almost as though Domilini had died or disappeared or something.

I came over to fix dinner that night, and was kind of stunned to see her curled up on the corner of the couch, her face red and splotchy like she'd been crying, her cheeks still wet. There was a book on the floor next to her.

"Drop your book, Edith?" I said, stooping to pick it up.

"Don't bother! I can't read anymore, God damn it!"

I didn't know what to say.

"You don't know," she went on. "This is terrible. I can't believe it. You have no idea what this is like. What the hell is a life without reading, or writing? It's a concentration camp, that's what it is! Damn it all to hell!"

Now the tears were flowing. She wasn't sobbing, but the tears were running down her cheeks and onto her lips. I tried to hand her the tissue box, but she swatted it out of my hand. It landed on the rug and skittered into the corner, like it was afraid of her.

She wriggled her way along the couch, then stood up on her own for what seemed like the first time in weeks. She hadn't been upstairs since the time she fell and broke a rib, more than a year ago, but she was clearly headed that way.

I asked her where she was going.

"I'm going to get my gun," she said. Her voice was matter-of-fact, as though she was going to put on a pot for tea. "I'm going to shoot myself."

She was crawling, now, toward the stairway, and had managed to pull herself up so that her torso was on the first step and the rest of her was sprawled down on the floor. She was struggling to get her knee up to join her hands.

Edith did actually have an ancient little .22 pistol in her bedroom. Or I should say, used to have a pistol. I'd already found it and gotten it out of there. There's no point in having a gun around if you don't have to.

I didn't tell her that, though. There didn't seem any point in that, either. I guess she had the gun for protection, and even though she'd never be able to get to it if she needed to, believing it was there probably made her feel a little more comfortable, and I suppose there was no harm in that.

Edith was cursing a blue streak, and still had only made it up two steps to the landing where the stairs made a left-hand turn. I didn't try to stop her, but I didn't go to help her, either. Whatever was happening in this moment, I needed to let it happen. There was nothing I could do to make Edith feel better, and nothing I could do that wouldn't make her feel worse. I just had to sit there and watch this old woman struggling to get up a flight of stairs that she couldn't climb, to find a gun that wasn't there.

Edith had made it to the third step when she gave up. She was crying again, but seemed as mad as she was unhappy. A terrible thought flashed through my mind: I realized that I could, in fact, let her have the gun and do what she wanted. There's no future for her, she's in such torment, and why shouldn't a person have the right to decide what day they cross over to the other side? When did we all get together and decide that no one gets to make that choice?

It was a horrible thought, and before it became too graphic

and real for me I pushed it out of my mind, and turned my attention back to the moment, to Edith, crying on the stairs. I got up and walked over to her, and sat down on the steps, and gave her a hug.

"C'mon, let's go back downstairs," I said.

Edith didn't say anything, but she let me help her up and back onto the couch. I found the frightened little box of tissues and put it back on the coffee table. I was making my way to the kitchen when I stopped and turned to Edith, because I thought she might want to talk, but she just sat there, staring at the TV but not seeing it. I realized that there was, really, nothing for either of us to say.

It was about a week before I broached the subject again of going to the hospital for all the tests she'd been avoiding. I didn't know what was wrong with her, but I knew something was up. No one could eat as much as I was feeding that woman and keep losing weight. There were no really bad symptoms, outside of a pretty frequent tummyache and the fact that she was peeing fifty times a day, but clearly something was out of whack.

Edith finally agreed to another trip up to Pill Hill. She was feeling so weak, and had been saying she wanted to go back into physical rehabilitation, thinking it might help her get her strength back, and I realized there was my in. I couldn't talk her into doing things if she didn't want to; but if I could start from Point A of what she wanted to do, I could get to Point B of what I thought she needed to do.

I reminded her that if she'd go to the hospital and submit to the X-ray and MRI and whatnot, that the doctor could prescribe rehab, and then Medicare would pay for it. That did the trick. She told me to go ahead and schedule it.

I called up and got an appointment for the following Monday. I wanted to do this soon, before Edith had a chance to change her mind.

I told her that I thought she'd better go in an ambulance this time, since it was getting so hard for her to get around. Truth is, I figured if she was in an ambulance it would be harder for her to change her mind when she got a block away from the place. It worked.

Monday came, and when I finished up at the construction site I drove to the hospital. There was a bicycle rack out front, packed to the gills with bikes, and I wondered, who the heck rides their bike to go to the hospital? But of course the bikes must have belonged to staff members, and they put the rack right out front there to show how environmentally conscious they were. People in Seattle are like that.

My next thought, funnily enough, was of Edith riding a bicycle. I tried to imagine her as a young woman. She must have ridden a bicycle; didn't everyone back in those days? Or is that just some image you have from old postcards? I thought of her riding a bicycle in Paris, or in Germany. I tried to picture her the way she was in that photo with the clarinet, riding her bike over to her cousin Benny Goodman's house. In my imagination her hair was long and blowing in the breeze, and she was smiling, without a care in the world.

The sun was just going down as I walked toward the big

curved metal awning of the hospital entrance; it was still getting pretty chilly in the evenings, and I could see my breath in front of me as I passed a little clutch of men in coats and blue hospital pants, smoking off to the side, a respectable distance from the automatic doors. I had to stop and wait for the doors to slide open, and then stand aside as another man in a coat and hospital blues wheeled an old man out toward a waiting car. My feet felt heavy, all of a sudden. I realized that in all the effort it had taken to get Edith here, I hadn't thought much about what they might find out. Now that I was about to learn what it was, I wasn't at all sure I was ready for it. But it was silly to just stand there, and as soon as the man in the wheelchair passed, I walked on in.

It was like a furnace inside the hospital, and the heat made me feel even more tired than I already was. I shook it off, though, and found the information desk, where they told me Edith had been admitted to stay overnight. I don't know why I was surprised by that, but I guess I hadn't thought that part through either. I headed for her room.

When I got off the elevator, I saw the nurses' station right down the hallway, so I figured I'd check in there first. As soon as I told the nurse who I was, I could see her stiffen up a bit. I knew something was up.

"It's not good," she told me straight out. "She has pancreatic cancer."

Just like that.

I guess it was better that she said it flat out, without beating around the bush. It goes right into your brain, and finds the place where you were thinking that it might be something like that, even if you hadn't admitted it to yourself. I guess when a woman reaches eighty-six years old, and you're spending most of every day with her, you've got to at least consider the possibility of what she might be facing. And I realized, as she said the word, *cancer*, that I'd thought it a few times, but I must have just banished the thought from my mind, like I'd banished the thought of giving her a gun. Edith was so strong, so self-assured, so in control, that I guess I never really thought to look around that particular corner. Or maybe I just didn't want to. Because, to be perfectly blunt about it, I had come to love Edith in a way that was as important to me as the love I had for my own family. When you love someone like that, a part of your brain just shuts down, the part that doesn't want to see what it doesn't want to see, doesn't want to hear what it doesn't want to hear.

But now I heard it, standing there in the fluorescent light, and the word hung in the air, in front of me, like I could see it sitting there.

Cancer.

I don't know how long I was standing there, just letting the thought sink in, but the nurse was patient—I'm sure this wasn't the first time she'd had to break the news to someone—and she just looked at me, without pity or emotion, just waiting. The first words out of my mouth, after what seemed like forever, were "Does she know yet?"

"Yes, she knows," she said. "The social worker was in to see her, and explained it all to her." The nurse gave me a quick rundown of where things stood. Apparently Edith had three choices: Surgery, which was an iffy proposition at best for an eighty-six-year-old woman. It might do some good, but it could certainly do a lot of harm. Radiation and chemo were options, but not great ones, since she probably wasn't capable of withstanding the treatment. The third choice was to just let the disease run its course. That was the phrase she used— "run its course." My mind immediately went to the end of that course, but it was a place I couldn't quite let myself fathom, just yet.

I thanked the nurse and walked down to Edith's room. She was sharing it with another patient, and the TV was on a little too loud, but I was used to talking to Edith over the sound of the television, so it didn't seem inappropriate.

I just said, how are you doing, and she just said, fine, and we chatted for a few minutes about nothing, about the details of the day, both of us waiting for the other to raise the subject, I guess.

"So, do you know what's going on? Did they tell you?" I finally asked her.

"Yes," she said. "Yes, they did," and she turned away, to look at the television.

She seemed so small in that hospital bed, in that flimsy robe, behind the big metal bars on the bedside. She was holding in her hand the remote that controlled the bed and the TV and called the nurse, and her hand seemed so tiny around that big device. Something about the light of a hospital room makes everything seem a little surreal, like you could close your eyes and open them and be back at home like none of this ever happened. Or maybe you just want it to look like that.

We talked a little bit about the options the nurse had told me about, the chemo and surgery and all, and of course Edith said she didn't want to do any of those things. I started to argue with her—but then I stopped.

What would she get out of fighting this thing? I know what I would get out of it. I would get the satisfaction of knowing I'd done everything I could for her. But Edith Wilson Macefield, what was in it for her? Certainly not any quality of life. It would take her too long to recover, if she recovered at all. My mind flashed back once again to the conversation we'd had, when I first met her, about the Kingdome. How change didn't really bother her, because everything changes eventually; the building I was putting up would be torn down, just like they tore down the Kingdome twenty years after they built it. A little fragment of a song from who knows where floated through my head—just a snippet, something about "it's just the way it changes, like the shoreline and the sea." I looked down at Edith, and as strange as it is to say, she seemed relaxed. Relieved, even.

I couldn't put my finger on it. I suppose it could have been the drugs they'd given her, but I didn't think so. It seemed like more than that—that there was something about the day that had changed her in a way I hadn't expected.

I pulled up the little plastic chair next to her bed, and sat down.

"Did they give you any dinner, Edith?" I asked her.

"Tried to. It was horrible. I'd rather starve than try to eat the slop in this joint."

Well, I thought, at least Edith is still Edith. I told her I'd go down the hall and see what they had in the machines.

As I went foraging, I felt the weight of the new knowledge settle over me, like I could almost feel its physical presence: cancer. It's not like I thought Edith was going to live forever, but the reality of this, the simple fact of it, felt like we were on a train that had switched over to a different track. There was no going back. There was only riding this to the end of the line.

The thought reminded me of something a friend of mine used to like to say: Be careful of that light at the end of the tunnel. It might be a train that's headed right for you. But I thought, That's not really what Edith's going through—or what I'm going through. In fact, it's just the opposite. For a long time, Edith had been in a long, dark tunnel, unable to read, to write, to control her bodily functions, and there was no end in sight and no explanation for it. Now there was a reason for it, a name for it, and that, at least, shed some light into this dark, dark tunnel.

I stopped walking, right in the middle of the hallway, because the thought hit me like someone had thrown a tennis ball at my forehead. This, I realized, was exactly what my father went through when he was diagnosed with Alzheimer's.

I thought about the two of them: *Alzheimer's. Cancer.* Not the most pleasant words that can come into your life. But the words themselves have so much meaning, so much weight, and are such double-edged swords. I don't mean to downplay them in any way, but part of what I was learning, from Edith, day by day, was how to deal with my father and his illness. And part of the lesson, in this moment, in the relaxed look I had seen on Edith's face, was simply this: that the not-knowing is the worst. I'd heard John Walsh on *America's Most Wanted* say that a bunch of times, when he was talking about missing children, but I'd never really understood it until this moment. The not-knowing is the worst. For Edith, the darkness she'd been living in had been lifted. Even though it revealed a horrible, terrible, life-threatening truth, at least she knew, now, what the world held for her. She always needed to know, I realized, what was happening: Was I coming at six or seven? Was I sleeping on her floor tonight or going home? Who was going to take care of her on the weekend that I was out of town? Those, and a thousand other details, were the essentials of her life. It always bugged me when she'd grill me with questions: What time are you coming? What time are we having dinner? What time are you leaving? And I'd think, kind of annoyed, Well, why, are you going somewhere? But really, when I thought about this moment, it made perfect sense. Of course she always needed to know the tiny details of the day—it was her way of feeling at least a little bit in control. And of course she needed to argue about all of them— because that was her way of exerting some of that control.

And so it would make sense for her to feel relaxed, even confident, after finding out she'd gotten The Big C, as paradoxical as it might seem. Because the not-knowing had made this the one part of her life that she had had no control over; but now she was the boss again. Chemo? Radiation? Surgery? If nothing else, she got to make the decisions, the big, big decisions. That is the one thing that diminishes as you get older—and the one thing that those of us who help out need to remember. They've spent their lives making enormous decisions about their own destiny, and the destinies of others. If even half of what Edith had told me about her past was true, she had made decisions that affected the very lives of dozens of children. So to be given, one last time, the power over life and death—the power to choose, to decide—must be a very deeply reassuring feeling. More reassuring than life itself, I guess.

There was only junk food in the machines—which always surprises me, in a hospital, a place that's supposed to be all about making you healthy, that the machines are so filled with crap. And then I laughed at myself again. "Well," I thought, as I slid in a dollar and pushed the button for some kind of cake-type device, "it's not like it's gonna kill her."

13

Edith's cancer diagnosis was so devastating, that the second wave of bad news, when it came, didn't even seem like that big a deal in the grand scheme of things.

Diabetes.

No wonder she was peeing like a racehorse. It all made sense. I resisted the urge to beat myself up for not making her come for the tests sooner. I tried to focus on the fact that now, at least, there was some relief coming. There might be nothing we could do about the cancer, but at least we could treat the diabetes. As far as I could tell, that was going to be the biggest thing to make her more comfortable. As the days dwindle down, you take the little victories you can get.

Or so I thought.

The nurses gave Edith insulin while she was in the hospital, along with the other medications, which was why she wasn't guzzling gallons of water or peeing every fifteen minutes. It was a hell of a relief to have an answer to all that, and to know that we at least had something under control.

And Edith was pretty happy to be getting out of the hospital and going back to her little house. I couldn't blame her. A hospital is no place for a sick person. Of course, there was a mountain of paperwork to go through. I expected that. As a matter of fact, I was pretty proud of how good I was getting at taking care of all of Edith's hospital forms, paperwork, and prescriptions. I knew what to look out for and, as much as anybody can, to spot what was missing.

What was missing this time was a prescription for insulin. And as I thought about it, no one had talked to me about how the hell you take care of a diabetic anyway.

I had to wait about two hours to see the doctor, but when he finally came, I asked him to step outside the room—I pretended it was because the television was too loud, but Edith didn't seem all that interested anyway. When we were standing in the hallway, I asked him what we were going to do about the diabetes.

"Mister Martin," he said—I knew it was gonna be bad news as soon as he called me Mister Martin—"we have to set a treatment for the pancreatic cancer first."

He told me that we could do nothing, or try chemo, or surgery—the same la-di-da I'd heard about a half-dozen times now. I told him, as I'd told everyone else, that she had decided not to do any of those things. What I wanted was to make her comfortable.

"Mister Martin," he said again—I was starting to get pissed

off every time I heard him say my name—"diabetes is not going to kill her."

Neither is a Hostess Twinkie, I thought. But that's not the point.

"Look," I said, surprised a little at how angry I sounded. "I know that as a doctor you're looking at the big disease and you want to go after it because that's what you do. But that's not what Edith wants to do. Now, we can't 'manage' cancer but we can manage diabetes, so I will ask you again, what are we going to do about the diabetes?"

The doctor stared at me for a second. I don't think doctors like being challenged, and it seemed like he was deciding whether or not to walk away.

"She can't manage her own condition. She can't check her blood sugar. She can't give herself a shot," he said, in a tone that indicated he felt like that was the end of the conversation, and any sane person would recognize it.

"Maybe she can't," I said. "But I can."

And he says, "Oh, really. How much time do you have?"

And I say, "As much as it takes."

And he says, "Well, do you know how to give her a shot?"

And I say, "No, but somebody could show me. You know it's not rocket science."

And he says, "Well, you know, but then you've got to test her blood sugar."

And I say, "Okay, how often do you have to do that?"

"Well, once a day."

"Okay. I can do that."

"Well, you know, how often are you there?"

"I'm there all day, all night, and all weekend. That work for you?"

And he says, "Okay, keep talking. You're convincing me."

That pissed me off even more. Why did I have to convince him? He not the one who should be making the decision. Edith is. And I'm the one talking for Edith. But I knew I was turning the tide, so I just kept focused.

"You told me that this was all about trying to make things as easy or as best they can be, with what she's got," I said. "Having to pee forty-five times a day and drinking all this water isn't all that comfortable. She's getting sores on her butt from sliding onto the commode. I can help her so she doesn't have to do that. *You* can help her so she doesn't have to do that. It's not that big a deal."

That seemed to get the ball over the goal line. "Okay," the doctor said. "You convinced me. Wait here."

I didn't have to wait more than two seconds. The doctor grabbed the nearest nurse and told her to give me a crash course in managing diabetes. The nurse was cool and efficient about it all, explaining to me how to test for blood sugar and how to give someone a shot like she was explaining how to change a flat tire. The instruction session took all of about five and a half minutes, and the next thing you know, Edith was in a wheelchair, headed for the door, with me walking next to her, with a prescription for insulin folded neatly in my wallet.

I filled Edith in on my conversation with the doctor as we drove home. She just kind of grinned. I think she liked that I was giving him hell. She actually thanked me for standing up for her, and for agreeing to manage the diabetes. But other than that we didn't talk much. I think she was trying to show that she was tough. "So what's for dinner?" she asked, and that was about that. I was kind of lost in thought, driving by rote, like a mule following its path back to the barn. I was kind of surprised when we turned onto Edith's block, like someone else had driven us there. I got Edith settled in, and then went back out to the pharmacy.

I handed the prescription to the girl behind the counter with a little sense of pride, like I was showing off a report card full of A's. While I was waiting, I thought, of all the lessons I'd learned through this whole cockamamie process, this one—the idea of not just accepting what the doctors told you, but learning to speak up for yourself and your loved ones—was probably the one that would come in the most handy when I'd have to really start dealing with my dad. And that piece of paper was a symbol of that lesson. I half wanted to ask for it back and take it home and frame it. I guess I've always been a little feisty when it comes to doctors, but I'd never had a real reason to confront one before. What do people do when there's no one to be an advocate for them? Especially when you're in the hospital, all doped up, and not feeling that good to begin with, your mind's not at all clear, and these too-busy doctors come rushing in and tell you what they want to tell you and rush back out before you can take a breath. Edith probably didn't know she was getting insulin in the hospital. They may have told her, but it might have been a nurse who came in at six o'clock in the morning—did Edith process that information? I felt lucky that I was there, and had the wherewithal, to fight on Edith's behalf. And I felt damn glad that I won, that's for sure.

Even Edith, bulldog that she was, would not have had that fight, if she even knew to have it. I doubt she would have won it in any case. She probably would have walked out of there without the prescription that was my trophy. The prescription, more important, that was going to make a difference in Edith's life. A huge difference.

This was the lesson for today, class, I thought to myself. It's not enough just to show up. You have to show up ready to fight.

It was awkward, the first time I had to give Edith a shot of insulin. "Be careful," she snapped as I got everything ready. "You don't know what the hell you're doing. Why don't you get someone in here who's at least a little competent?" I just shrugged it off.

I went through the little routine that they had shown me at the hospital. First I took the device they gave me to poke Edith's finger with, just enough to give her a little pinprick and produce a tiny drop of blood. I put that blood on a strip of paper and inserted it into another device, an electronic gadget a little smaller than a cell phone, that gave me a readout with her blood sugar level.

Then I got one of the small glass insulin bottles out of the refrigerator, the ones with the little rubber tops, and cleaned it with an alcohol wipe. I inserted the needle, turned it upside down, and filled the needle.

Showtime.

I wiped the back of Edith's arm with another alcohol wipe, took a deep breath, and stuck the needle in. The whole thing went fine, to my surprise, and, I think, to Edith's.

I gave her the shot every day before breakfast, but after a week, when I inserted the needle, she flinched. "Damn, that hurt!" she said. "You're hurting me, dammit!" I couldn't figure out what I was doing differently. Was her arm getting that much more tender? This went on for a few days—every day, the same thing. Edith was getting more and more frustrated, and so was I.

Finally, I realized what was going on. I'd gotten so good at this that I'd gone into hurry-up mode. Like with everything else, I was trying to be accurate and efficient—get in, give her the shot, fix breakfast, clean the commode, make sure she was set for the morning, get out—so quick, in fact, that I wasn't giving the alcohol rub enough time to dry before I put the needle in. So I was actually injecting alcohol into her arm, and it stung like hell. The next day, I took a little more time, and we were back to normal. So was her blood sugar. When I left that morning to walk the twenty-nine steps to my trailer, I felt like a hurricane had passed. It left a lot of devastation behind, but for now, at least, the sky was clear, the air was calm, and things were relatively peaceful and quiet.

It was a busy time at work. Ever since we'd had the problem with the high-tension wires, it seemed like everything we did had to be worked out twice—the way we originally planned it, and the way we had to replan it to work around the wires. As I said, we were creating a kind of zigzag-shaped building, as you looked at it from ground level, stair-stepping the higher floors to avoid the high-tension wires. It looked like we were building a staircase for the high-tension pole to walk up. But stair-stepping the higher floors was much, much more complicated than it might sound. It wasn't just a matter of doing less construction. Because for every floor you go up you also have to consider your electrical wires and plumbing and ventilation, which meant that every single step of that had to be reconfigured while we waited for the high-tension-wire process to work itself out. The electrical wires didn't reach all the way to the edge of the building anymore, so how would we deal with that? And the floors on one side of the building were not designed to carry all the weight that we were about to put on them. That meant we had to tighten the cables that went through the floor below. But we couldn't tighten the cables, because we couldn't complete the floor until the high-tension wires were moved. So I wound up having to go all the way back down to the basement to add additional shoring that would allow me to stair-step the other floors without the whole thing collapsing. And every issue we solved created new problems that needed solving.

I suppose that's why I was rushing a lot when I was at Edith's. My mind was pretty consumed with work. I found myself lying in bed at night trying to re-sequence the progression of the job, or wondering how the engineers were coming on reconfiguring electrical wiring and calculating weight ratios, and had to find a way to force myself to think about something else.

And then, one night, my mind drifted back to Edith's past. It was still like a puzzle where all the pieces didn't fit together. I kept thinking of ways I could look stuff up about Edith's past on the Internet, but I wouldn't jump up out of bed and go to the computer, and the next morning I would forget all about it. Then I'd tell myself to leave a pad next to the bed, but by the next night I'd forget about that, too.

But the questions about Edith's past were bubbling up for me, and I found myself more and more curious.

One Saturday night in early March, after I'd finished the dinner dishes and come back into the living room, I was surprised to find that the TV wasn't on. Edith never, ever turned the TV off, so I wondered what was up.

"TV on the blink, Edith?" I asked.

"No, I was just thinking," she said. She was looking out the window. It was almost dark now, but her house faced south, so if you sat on the couch and looked out to the right you could see the part of the sky that got dark the latest. Edith was staring over there, like she was trying to find the last bit of light in the sky.

"What were you thinking about?"

She didn't turn to look at me. "Richard," she said.

I thought to myself, well la-di-da, I guess I'm not the only one thinking about her past. It was the first time I could re-member her ever bringing up the past on her own, without my prompting her. I suppose when you're confronted with a big diagnosis like the one Edith had just been hit with, tough as you might want to be, you can't help but think about the past, and the people who've been important to you. It's only natural.

The kettle started to whistle, so I went into the kitchen to get us both a cup of tea. There was a string of handmade bells hanging in the doorway, and every time I'd go back and forth I'd brush them and they'd ring a little bit. For some reason I had never asked before, but something about this night, about what we'd been through lately, made me raise the question.

"Where are those bells from?" I asked her as I set her tea down on the coffee table. "Old family heirloom?"

Edith turned toward me, but she didn't answer right away. It was like she had her hand on a doorknob and was trying to decide whether to turn it and open the door.

And the next thing I knew, she flung it wide.

"They're from a camel," she said. "From James's plantation."

It was like there were three questions in my head fighting to see which one could get to my mouth first—

Camel?

Plantation?

James?

Before I could say another word, Edith did something Edith never did. She told me a story, start to finish.

And what a story it was.

It seems that after she escaped from the concentration camp, Edith had traveled around a bit, through Austria, and back to Germany. Richard Tauber showed back up in her life, and they began an affair. They got married, Edith said, and lived for a short time as man and wife, until Edith got pregnant.

Richard and Edith decided that with all that was going on

in the world, the child would not be safe unless it had a pure name. I was a little confused by what she meant by *pure*; I didn't learn until later that Tauber was part Jewish, and had been assaulted by Nazis because of it.

To ensure the child's safety, Edith left Richard and moved to England, where the child was born. There, she became reacquainted with a man she knew named James Macefield, a well-to-do widower with older children. They married—even though Edith was already married—but their marriage was purely platonic, more a marriage of convenience for both of them. He gave her a home and a name for her child. She gave him companionship and—well, I'd known Edith long enough to imagine how she could draw someone in with her stories. And I'd heard enough of those stories to know that she had the ability to charm men when she wanted to.

James Macefield had a plantation in Africa, and they spent many months at a time there. She told me about the time she made fruit pies and put them on the windowsill to cool, and the giraffes came up to the compound, stuck their heads over the wall, and ate the pies off the sill.

Edith laughed at the memory; I think it was the first time I ever heard her laugh when she told me one of her stories. She took a sip of her tea and looked out the window. It was dark now, and I was afraid she was going to stop the story right there, with the giraffes eating the pies. But she went on.

It was around that time that she was given the castle that became an orphanage. Richard Tauber would show up now and again, but the children didn't like him for some reason. She said she was still deeply, madly in love with him. That's how she said it: deeply, madly. It felt a little like something a romance writer would say, and I thought about those books on her desk and wondered how much of this story was in those books, or how much of those books was in the story I was hearing right now.

Eventually, Richard, who was twenty-five years older than Edith, took sick. He spent several long weeks in the hospital, and then he died. He died in that hospital bed with Edith looking on. Well, she couldn't take it, she said. The heartache was too great. She ran out of the hospital and asked God to erase Richard Tauber from her memory. She never went back to the hospital—she asked some friends to take care of the arrangements—and she didn't go to his funeral, either. In fact, she continued, she hadn't thought about him at all, until a few years ago when she finally allowed herself to buy his CDs, the ones she listened to every night the minute I walked out the door.

When she was done, she picked up her teacup and slurped the last sip. "That was good tea," she said. "It was decaf, right? You wouldn't give me regular tea, I know. I have enough trouble sleeping as it is. You take pretty good care of me, I have to say."

I assumed that was her signal that she didn't want to talk about her past anymore and wasn't taking any questions. It was getting pretty late anyway. I got up to leave, and made sure everything was in its place, and gave her a little kiss on the forehead.

"I'll be listening for your key in the door," she said.

As I walked out, I happened to notice the picture of Edith

holding the clarinet that she said Benny Goodman had given her, sitting on the table with that lamp from my childhood. It felt so odd. These little physical objects, a table, a lamp, a clarinet; so meaningless, really. Just dumb stuff. But in another way, they were what tied us all together. Edith and her cousin—if he was really her cousin—connected by that clarinet. Edith and her mother, by those little Red Rose Tea figurines. Me and Edith, by that table, that lamp. When I went out to my truck, I saw that CD of Richard Tauber that I had borrowed, sitting on the front seat next to me, along with the pompoms from my daughter's competitive cheerleading that she'd left the night before. I thought, they're just some crappy shreds of plastic all tied together. But maybe one day she'll have a daughter of her own, and those will be the most important memories she'll have of her mom. She'll hang them on a wall, or frame them, or something. I shrugged and put the car in gear and thought, what a hoot. No wonder people become hoarders. It's all about what you throw away, and what you keep forever.

As I drove home, it started spitting a little, just lightly, like the sky couldn't decide if it felt like sending rain or snow. When I got home, dinner was long over. At least everyone was still awake—a lot of nights lately, I wasn't getting home until well after midnight. When I walked in, Evie was upstairs, watching TV. We didn't TiVo or DVR anything—still don't—so she'd just watch whatever was on. The kids were downstairs, doing their homework. I went to the fridge, took my dinner out to warm it up, and sat at the table, alone, lost in my thoughts.

14

My dad disappeared again. This time he had gone for a walk with the dog on a trail near his house, a trail that follows along under the power lines. He hadn't come back. We went through the same drill we'd gone through the last time—everybody calling each other all day, checking to see if he'd shown up at anyone's house. My mother had talked to the neighbors, and they'd convinced her to call search and rescue.

They were all out there at the top of the trail, their red and blue lights flashing. A bunch of neighbors were out there too, organizing search parties. The sun was getting ready to go down, so there was a real sense of urgency about it. One of the search-and-rescue guys had pulled out a map of the area, and it sounded like they were parceling out sections of ground for various people to cover. And just as all the commotion was going on, Dad comes hiking out of the woods, looking at all the emergency personnel with, as far as you could tell, no idea that they had anything to do with him. My mother went up to him and started yelling. He tried to pass it off like it was nothing. He'd gotten off the trail, he said, and it just took him a while to find his way back.

"You got yourself lost!" my mother yelled.

"I wasn't lost. The dog knew her way home," he said. That was about it, for Dad. But not for Mom.

I went up the next day to check on everybody, and my mother was still fit to be tied. My dad was in the living room, watching TV and drinking juice. I don't know what kind of talk I would have had with him before I met Edith, but after all I'd been through, I knew a little better how to approach it.

"So, I hear you had a nice little hike yesterday," I told him. He kind of grinned at me, like he knew he was caught doing something he shouldn't have.

"You know, a guy with Alzheimer's probably needs to make better decisions than that," I said. I was really careful to talk about him making decisions—not like we were going to make any decisions for him.

I think he got that, too. As we talked, and he agreed that he wouldn't take the dog for any more walks on that trail by himself, it felt like he was deciding that on his own. Now, whether he'd remember making that decision, or whether he'd stick by it, that was something we'd find out day by day, I guess. But for that day, for that moment, I thought, well, what do you know. Maybe this doesn't have to be as hard as everyone makes it out to be.

And for the second time, sitting with my dad, I thought: Thanks, Edith.

• • •

The next morning, when I told Edith about what had happened with my dad, she just smiled. "He's a tough old bird, from what you tell me," she said. "He can take care of himself." She meant my dad, but she really could have been talking about herself.

I made the sloppy toast and brought it in to her. It was going to be a long morning at work, and I knew I wouldn't be able to check back in until lunchtime, so I figured I'd sit for a minute before I took off. "Not rushing out of here as usual, huh?" Edith said.

"Why, are you trying to get rid of me?" I shot back.

She smiled again. "No, you know I'm always quite happy for your company," she said. It was odd, that formal way she had of talking, especially when she was trying to say something nice.

"You know," she said to me, "some mornings I miss Boris. He was only thirteen when he died, you know. You can't imagine what it is to lose a child."

I was blown away. She'd mentioned her son, of course, a bunch of times, but I never had heard what happened to him. And now she just drops this, right in the middle of the sloppy toast.

"How did he die?" I asked. It was all I could think of to say.

"Spinal meningitis. Hell of a thing."

"Where was this, Edith?"

But I could see that she didn't want to take it any further, and I knew better than to press. "This is good sloppy toast," she said.

That night, the door opened up again. She was in the mood to talk, I guess. Maybe the cancer made her realize that she didn't have all the time in the world, and if she was ever going to tell anyone this story, it might as well be me. All I know is, I always had to tug and tug to get two words out of her when it came to the past, and now this stuff was just pouring out. Stories I'd wondered about for a year.

Without much prompting, Edith started telling me the one story that I questioned the most.

But then again, who would make up a story about being in a concentration camp?

It was after dinner, and Edith wasn't mincing any words. She said that back when she was in Germany, someone had accused her of being a spy, and that same afternoon she was on a train to Dachau, thrown into a barracks with dozens of Jewish children. "I know the guard was molesting some of the children," Edith was saying. "Don't ask me how I know. I just know." It was a helluva thing to say, right out like that. I wondered if she meant that she was molested as well.

She didn't go into a lot of detail at this point, but she did say that one night, not long after she was put there, she heard a knock on the barracks door. She opened it and saw no one, at first. But when she looked around, she saw the guard, lying dead, facedown, just outside the entrance.

"My heart was in my throat," she said, and I couldn't help but think it sounded like a line from one of her novels again. I felt like I was hearing this in two ways—as a story she was remembering, and a story she was making up.

She went on: There was a laundry truck parked right near

the guard's body. She tiptoed over to it, wondering why no one else was around. She saw that the keys were in the truck and there were directions, on the seat, about how to escape.

Edith said she wasted no time. She went into the barracks and rounded up thirteen of the children, as many as she thought she could fit, and herded them into the back of the truck.

The children were silent, she said, and their eyes were wide. Edith couldn't have been more than twenty-one, and here she was, leading an escape from a concentration camp. I couldn't believe my ears.

"I realized that it had to be Hitler who arranged my escape," Edith said. "I think he took a liking to me. Do you remember he introduced me to a young blond-haired boy? Later he would bring the boy to me and ask me to take him to England and watch over him. I think that was his own son, believe it or not. I think he trusted me, and wanted me to take care of that boy. I think that's why he arranged my escape."

I was really finding this part hard to believe. I mean, really—Hitler's son? The concentration camp? But then, in the next minute, as she picked back up on the story of the escape, Edith's eyes got misty with tears, and I thought, she can't be making this up: "After we had gone a little ways, I decided to leave the truck behind, because I thought maybe someone would follow us. What if they changed their minds? What if whoever let us go didn't have the authority, and now they were going to come for us? So we set off on foot. Across the Alps. Barefoot."

It was cold, she said. The children's feet were bleeding, and she tore off pieces of their clothing and tied them to their feet. Most of the children survived that night, she said.

Most of them.

She was sobbing now, and could barely get the words out. Two of them died.

That was all she could say, and to be frank, that was all I could hear.

We started talking about something else, something mundane. I can't remember what it was; I just know that Edith had that ability to change the subject and talk about something else, like nothing had ever happened. It felt afterward like I had dreamed the whole conversation. Only I knew I hadn't.

I also knew that, unless she brought it up herself, I wasn't going to ask her any more about it.

Were these stories true? Was she making the whole thing up? That could matter to only one person. Me. It didn't help Edith one bit if I figured out whether she was married to Richard Tauber, or to a guy who owned a plantation in Africa, or whether she really got married again later in life and her husband died on their honeymoon; whether Hitler arranged her escape from the worst concentration camp in Germany, or whether she'd spent the war years in a loony bin and I'm the guy she found when she escaped.

If I was going to be the guy I thought I was, the guy who was a true friend, and—well, steadfast, really—then I was going to have to accept Edith for who she was. Someone who had changed my life by allowing me to see that the world was much, much larger than I ever imagined it to be.

Edith had given me the chance to be a better person. She

opened up my world, and challenged me to do the right thing. And I wanted to do the right thing, for her, not for me, even if sometimes that meant just listening, and really hearing.

After I finished cleaning up that evening, when I gave her her kiss on the forehead and went to leave, I noticed as I closed the door behind me how solid it was, now. She had called the aid car so many times, and they'd broken that door down so many times, and I'd repaired it so many times, that at some point I just decided to rebuild it from scratch. I used some left-over materials I had at the construction site, and got a good solid lock from Home Depot, and now, as I closed it, I heard a whoosh of air coming out, as though I'd built it perfectly airtight. It was a secure and calming feeling, the feeling of closing that door.

I swung up onto the ramp leading to the highway, and turned on the radio. I forgot that I'd put one of Edith's CDs in. I clicked on my turn signal to merge into traffic, and for a second it sounded like it was keeping time with the music. And damn if it wasn't Richard Tauber, singing that song Edith loved so much: "Long ago, and far away, I dreamed a dream one day . . ."

I pulled into traffic, and settled in with Richard Tauber for the journey home.

15

If you're going to be honest when you tell the story of what it takes to take care of an old person, then you have to admit that it takes a certain amount of lying.

I didn't particularly like lying to Edith, but I didn't particularly like not having any life whatsoever, either. So when I wanted to get away with my buddies once in a while, maybe I didn't exactly tell Edith the truth about where I was going. So sue me.

For example, a little while after I started taking care of Edith pretty much full-time, I had to take an OSHA safety class. The state doesn't require them, but most of the outfits you work for like it if you've taken those classes and have those credentials, because then if something goes wrong on the job site, they can say, well, we've taken all the safety measures you can take, including hiring a guy who has taken all the OSHA classes. Some firms you work for, including Ledcor, even require it. For me, I also liked knowing what was considered the safest operating procedure, because ultimately I'm responsible for the health and safety of everybody on the job site; and not to make too much of it, but that's a pretty darn big responsibility.

It was the previous spring that I told Edith I had to go off and take the class. She seemed to accept that. Evie and my daughter and a friend of Evie's came over to her place while I was away, and it was good to get a little break.

So this spring, some buddies were headed down onto the Columbia River to fish for springers. Springers are king salmon. They hit the river in the spring, and have the largest fat content of any salmon. And they just melt in your mouth like butter. Every once in a while you can buy them in the store, but they're like $29 a pound. You know how many are running over the dam at Bonneville because the state keeps count, and when I heard how big they were running I had to figure out a way to get there. So I told Edith that I needed to take another OSHA course, and that was that.

Like I said, sometimes lying is just easier.

I could go to that well only so often, however. I did have to give up the shrimping season that spring. We didn't go clamming, either. But I sure wasn't going to give up Memorial Day if I could help it. It's another big family tradition of ours, to go up to Pearrygin Lake State Park. We go with a bunch of different families, and we've been doing it for fifteen years. I'd told Edith about it too many times to pretend there was an OSHA meeting that weekend, so I just started preparing her, about a month ahead of time, that I was going to be gone for a few days.

Things hadn't been going all that well, lately. As the weather got nicer, it seemed like Edith was going in just the opposite direction. Every day her world got a little smaller. She'd pretty much given up on writing; once in a while I'd still walk in and find her sitting at the chair in front of the Whisperwriter, trying to peck something out on the keyboard, and it was just painful to watch. I'm not sure what she was trying to write, but it was pretty clear that she wasn't going to get through it. Clear to me, anyway.

Then there was the sedation. They had given me some drugs that I could give her when the pain got too great. We were both kind of cautious about using them, but it seemed, that spring, that I was having to sedate her more and more often.

So with all that going on, I was feeling pretty trepidatious about my Memorial Day trip, as much as I was stubbornly clinging to the idea that I wasn't going to miss it. I think when you're taking care of an old person and everyone's telling you what a great sacrifice you're making, what you're really thinking is, it might seem that way, but I'm drawing this selfish little line in the sand, and come hell or high water I am not going to let this old lady cross it. Or drag me across it. For me, Memorial Day was that stubborn, selfish line in the sand. I'd done this every Memorial Day for more than fifteen years, and probably will the rest of my life, so I don't know why I was so dead set against missing it one time, but there it was.

The big question, of course, was who was going to take care of Edith while I was away. Edith's friend Gail would have stepped in to help, but she was out of town for the weekend.

Leslie, one of my neighbors, took pity on my plight, and said she'd step in for the weekend.

"How hard could it be?" she asked.

First off, we needed to have Edith meet Leslie, because if Leslie didn't get Edith's seal of approval, the whole thing wasn't going to work. We arranged a meeting on a Saturday, a couple of weeks before Memorial Day. It went about as well as you could expect. I showed Leslie all of the routines—how to make sure Edith had enough water, how to do the pills, and all that. When Edith was out of earshot, I told Leslie the little trick about pretending to preheat the oven for half an hour. I also told her to make sure Edith didn't take any extra pain medication. We'd just had to double the dose, because her pain was getting worse, and I was getting worried that she'd wind up overdosing, like she did with the sleeping pills. Who the heck knows where that could lead. I told Leslie to blame me—to tell Edith that Barry only left so many pills, and she didn't have any extras.

Edith really seemed to like Leslie, which was a big plus. Leslie, for her part, was intrigued by Edith, having heard me tell a few of the stories. So when Memorial Day came, I crossed my fingers and headed for the state park.

Somebody told me that John Lennon was the first one to say that life is what happens when you're busy making other plans. I don't know if that's true, but it sure was the theme of that weekend.

The calls started a few hours after we got to the lake, and

they never stopped. At first they were just petty things—where did I leave the denture liners, Edith wants to take an extra pain pill, that sort of thing. But as night fell the calls got more serious. Edith started doing the I-can't-breathe routine, and Leslie was freaking out. The calls tapered off for a while, but at 1:30 in the morning, my cell phone rang again. It was Leslie. She was beside herself—Edith was saying, again, that she couldn't breathe, and Leslie was about to call 911, but she decided to call me first.

I had her put Edith on the phone. "Just take a deep breath," I said in my most reassuring, trying-not-to-sound-pissed-off voice. "Leslie's there. I'm camping. Even if I left now I couldn't get there for five hours. So you're better off dealing with Leslie than trying to get me to come back."

"But you are coming back, aren't you?" Edith asked. Her voice sounded almost like a child's, and I realized what this was all about.

It's all about coming back, and not coming back.

Someone told me once that playing peekaboo with babies is exciting to them because it touches their fear of being abandoned. The mother or father disappears, and then reappears, smiling, and that's kind of reassuring. I don't know about that, but I know there was something going on with Edith—the fear of being abandoned—that really resonated with me, as a parent. You know, in your gut, that the best thing you can do for your kids is to just let them know that you're always going to be there for them, no matter what. And it took me a while to get it through my thick head, but that's the one thing Edith needed to know, as well. That whole question she used to raise, when she'd yell at me—"I knew you couldn't stick it out!"—was her complicated, old-lady way of dealing with a little-kid fear of being abandoned.

"Of course I'm coming back, old woman," I said. "I'm always coming back. I'm just off on a camping trip. I'll see you day after tomorrow. Now get some sleep."

The next thing I knew, it was morning. The grass was wet with the dew, the sun was climbing over the hills above the lake, and my cell phone wasn't ringing. I checked it: no messages. We got up and made breakfast, got out on the lake and caught some fish, brought them back to clean them, cooked them up for lunch; and still, no call. I figured this was either a good sign, or the two of them had killed each other. My curiosity got the best of me, so after lunch, I called.

"Everything's fine," Leslie told me. "We had a nice morning. We watched this movie, *Waltz Time*. You won't believe it—there's a guy who sings in that movie? It's Edith's first husband!"

"See if you can get her to tell you the story" is all I said. "It's a doozy."

The days after I got home were rough. The pain didn't seem to be subsiding as much after Edith took her medications, and it came back much more quickly. By the middle of the week, I told her we had to go back to the hospital. She tried to fight me on it, but for once I asked her, "Do this for me, not for yourself but for me, because I just can't do this on my own anymore."

It's a card you shouldn't play too often. You have to really be at that place. I was really there—and I guess Edith understood that. She gave in, and I had her in the hospital by that afternoon.

I wasn't so happy with what was going on in the hospital. They'd give her a shot of some stuff that would knock her out for eight, ten, sometimes twelve hours. You could have set off a bomb in that room and I don't think she would have woken up. And then, by the end of the weekend, they gave me a call that I could come get her.

I just about went through the roof. "What do you mean, come get her?" I shot back—then, realizing how loud I was talking, tried to tamp it down a notch.

But this is what happens when you're taking care of an elderly person in a lot of pain. You just feel, at some point, that the people in the hospital, or the doctor's office, good people that they might be, are just overwhelmed and too busy and aren't really paying attention, and that you've got to get their attention, and you've got to get it now.

Which is what I guess I decided to do at that moment.

"She's not okay to come home. She's not any better than when she walked into the place," I said. "You haven't figured how to manage the pain. Every time she starts to squawk you give her something to knock her out so you don't have to deal with it. Now, I'm not taking her home till you figure this out. All I know is to keep giving her more of the pain medication, and I don't know at what point I'm giving her so much I'm going to kill her. Now, I don't think that's a very good plan of attack. Can we agree that we need to do something else, or do I need to come down there and talk about this some more?"

There was silence on the other end of the line. I didn't know if that was a good or a bad thing. I was worried that maybe she'd hung up on me.

Finally, she spoke. "Sir, I think you need to speak to the charge nurse about this," the woman on the other end of the line said.

"Well, then I need to speak to the charge nurse."

A good twenty minutes on hold didn't get me anywhere. I was planning to go back that afternoon to see Edith anyway, so I figured I'd just deal with it when I got down there.

On the drive down, I had some time to think. What on earth do people do, I wondered again, who don't have someone to advocate for them like this?

What if Edith was just alone there?

Suddenly I had this overwhelming feeling—like a rush of energy, building up behind my eyes. For a second I thought I was going to have to pull over. It occurred to me how many coincidences had to have taken place for me to be here, in this time, right now.

What if the company I'd been working for hadn't gone out of business? What if the guys from that company hadn't gone to work for Ledcor, or hadn't called me? Or what if I had decided to stay with the other job I'd found, instead of coming to work for them? What if the permits for this job hadn't taken so long to clear, so that I wasn't setting up camp next to Edith's house right at the moment she needed me? Or what if we had put the construction trailer on the other side of the lot, so I wasn't right next to Edith's house? When I started to count up all the dominoes that had to fall, just right, for me to be in the right place, at the right time, it was overwhelming.

Overwhelming, because there was a big part of me, a growing part of me, that didn't feel like it was a coincidence.

Some people like to say that things happen for a reason. I've never been one of those people. I never was before, anyway. But the feeling that there was something else guiding all of this, moving all the pieces around, was hard to ignore. I'm not sure I was ready to give a name to that feeling, but I knew that it was the feeling that most people have when they think of God.

I took a swig from a water bottle I had sitting on the passenger seat. However it was that I came to this place, I was there now. And I had a job to do.

I had to go show a charge nurse exactly who she was dealing with.

The charge nurse was a lot younger than I expected her to be, and a lot nicer, as well. It was just what I thought: these folks have so many patients to deal with, they just develop systems for getting through it all—automatic by-the-book responses. But if you can grab their attention and get them to focus on your particular concerns, they're actually pretty clever, and really know their stuff.

Someone must have warned her I was coming, because she seemed aware of what I was going to say before I could say it. I got about halfway through my I'm-not-taking-her-home-until-you-figure-this-out speech when she started laying out the options for what we could do next.

It only took a day or two to figure it out.

They tried her on a morphine drip—one of those things where you hit the button and it gives you another dose. Edith was awake, mostly, when I saw her for the next day or two. She was doped up, I'll grant you, but awake and alert and not in pain, which was the main thing.

I took her home a few days later, and called the hospice care nurse to set up the morphine. She came with the whole shebang. A bag that went on a high pole, a small rectangular tan-colored machine with a few knobs on the front, and then the line that went to the port they'd placed in Edith's arm. Even with that port, the whole thing bothered her to no end, and even on the morphine she still had the gumption to try to tear it out. We wound up having to strap it on so that Edith couldn't fuss with it.

I'd already made up my mind that I'd have someone there twenty-four hours a day. I guess I could have had less help, just for the hours I wasn't there, but I was too worried about having to leave her alone, even for a minute, with that apparatus.

"We don't have a choice this time," I told Edith. "I don't care if you don't like the person or if you think they're lazy or they smell bad. We just have to have twenty-four-hour care now. End of story."

This was the first time I'd really tried to take a big decision out of her hands. I wondered if this was a slippery slope I was going down.

But I didn't think about it too much. It would just be morally wrong to leave an old woman alone with a morphine drip. I didn't know how much time she had left, but I was determined to make sure she wasn't in pain for any of it, and if I had to be a little authoritarian, well, that was the price we were both going to have to pay.

I looked at Edith, and she didn't speak, right away, and I noticed the tears starting to form in her eyes. I started to speak again, but couldn't think of what to say.

"So that's it, then," she said after what felt like a long time. "So now I'll have twenty-four-hour care and I won't see you anymore. That's it, then," she repeated.

I don't know if it would have been different if I were her actual son; I don't know if she would have had this fear of abandonment if we were flesh and blood. I guess some folks do, no matter what. We've all known grown children who put their parents in a nursing home and promise to visit every few days, and after a while the visits trail off, and if the parents are coherent enough to understand it, they must feel the same way Edith did. I couldn't imagine any of that, right in that moment. I couldn't imagine not being there, not making sloppy toast in the morning, not putting on Richard Tauber at night. I didn't know how to tell her that she had nothing to worry about. But I knew it was true, like I know my own name.

"Of course I'll be here, you crazy old woman," I said. "I haven't finished watching all of your movies yet."

Something in her eyes told me she understood what I was trying to say. "Do you want to watch one now?" she asked.

I fought the urge to look at my watch, and I fought the urge to think about all of the things I needed to do back at the trailer. I knew she'd fall asleep in just a few minutes, once the TV was on and the morphine hit. For all we'd been through together, I figured I could spare a few minutes.

"Let's put on *Waltz Time*," I said. "We haven't watched that one in a while."

"I just saw that with Leslie," she said. "Go see if you can find *Heart's Desire*."

Edith and I didn't talk about her will much, but one morning, when I was over there, she was being her ornery self; something went wrong—I can't remember if the sloppy toast wasn't just right, or I poked her wrong when I was giving her her shot, but something was a little out of whack, and she snapped, "You know, I'm paying you a lot to do all this, so the least you could do is get it right."

"You're not paying me a thing to do this," I snapped back.

"The hell I'm not. I'm leaving you everything, you son of a bitch."

I dropped whatever I was doing. I'd never counted to ten before in my life, but I decided I'd better take a minute before I said anything.

"Whoa, back up," I said. I actually heard my voice quivering, so I took a deep breath. "I was doing all this long before you put me in your will. I'm grateful that you did but I never asked you to, and if you want to take me out tomorrow, you go right ahead. I'm taking care of you either way, so you make up your own mind."

I don't think I ever saw Edith speechless before. But she didn't say a word. She just turned back to the TV, and we left it at that.

16

It was two years, almost to the day, since I'd first walked onto that construction site, but the mall was finally taking shape. The big crane had been in place for months, lowering the concrete forms down around the rebar, making a kind of sandwich to pour the concrete into to form the walls. Slowly but surely the walls went up, and we were getting ready to put the roofs on.

There was something sad about those late spring days. It continued to feel as though Edith was moving in the opposite direction of the world outside, as though life was appearing in the trees and the yard at the same time it was drifting away from Edith. She was still feisty, sometimes—she'd get pissed off at the intravenous contraption, and yank the needle out of her arm, and I had to have the hospice nurse come in and put it back. I got a cream from the hospital that actually knocked you out, and while I didn't like to use it, every now and then, when she'd be out of control and pulling the needle out of her arm, I'd tell her that she had a dry spot on her arm, and I'd rub the cream on, and it would put her out. You had to wear rubber gloves while you were doing it or you'd wind up on the floor yourself, but she never caught on. I thought, maybe I'm no better than those folks at the hospital who used to knock her out every time she'd squawk. But I tried to tell myself it was different.

You have to tell yourself a lot of things, when it gets this tough, or you'll never make it through.

In the evenings, when I was leaving, I'd always kiss her on the forehead and tell her I loved her. She wouldn't respond, but once in a while, if she was awake, just as I was closing the door I'd hear, "I love you, too."

What's funny is, as much as things were changing—she was out of it, a lot of the time, and she was kind of dopey some of the time when she was awake—there were some things that didn't change at all. She still barked orders at me, and complained if I didn't do something just right. Sometimes she was downright nasty. But I knew better, by now, than to rise to the bait. And I guess that was the most important lesson, in those days—those final days, although I never called them that, never really wanted to face that those were the final days. I'd come to understand that Edith was dealing with it in her own way, the way she'd dealt with everything else: a mixture of denial, anger, and perseverance that would get her through this moment, as it had gotten her through so many others. It was funny, I thought. For someone who's such a romantic—who wrote what I understood were such romantic stories, hundreds and hundreds of pages of them—she's so rooted in reality, so down to the here-and-now.

So steadfast.

Even with the twenty-four-hour help, I was over at Edith's as much as, or maybe more than, I ever was. Sometimes I'd see her cringe, and I'd reach over and hit the button on the morphine machine. I couldn't take my eyes off the machine for more than a few minutes—I was always worried that the meds would run out, or that the batteries would die, or whatnot. One night, when the pain got too tough, I whispered to her that it was okay for her to let go—to go be with her mother. That I would take care of everything. She didn't respond to that, but I know she heard me. I hoped she understood.

The hospice people came by once or twice; they weren't pushy at all, like the social services people had been. They were the living embodiment of the lesson I was still learning, that you need to let old people make their own choices: They just wanted to make sure we knew that if Edith wanted to be in a facility, that that option was open to her, and if she didn't, they'd make this as comfortable for her as they could. I got Edith to let them come in, at first, by telling her they were here to trim her nails and give her a pedicure. That's all they did at first. She liked that, and little by little they became more involved. They were the ones who were arranging to get the meds sent to the house, the ones who took care of bringing special bedding, and those adult diapers (Edith liked to call them "Grampers") and whatever else we needed. They'd come in, quietly take care of what they needed to take care of, check to make sure I was doing everything right (and God bless them for that), and then slip away. The nurse would usually stay on the other side of the room, and so even with all these comings and goings, Edith and I had a certain amount of privacy.

It was the eve of Father's Day, and I was already feeling guilty because I knew I'd spend most of that day at Edith's— not with my kids, and not with my dad either. I knew they'd all understand, and I guess that made me feel even guiltier.

But I had taken on a task. And once you take on a task, you either do it or you don't. These days there's lots of talk about motivation and feelings, and what goes on inside a person that makes them one way or another. I know that's a question that surrounded me and Edith through all of this, and a question that people still ask me to this day.

But really, it's all very simple. You figure out what the right thing is, and then you do that thing. You don't need to talk about it a lot. You don't need to think about it a lot.

You just do the thing.

And if you leave it at that, it's really not so hard.

It was getting late, and I knew Evie would have dinner ready pretty soon. Edith was snoring quietly on the couch. The nurse was reading a paperback book. I checked the IV and the meds for the hundredth time that day, and leaned over and gave Edith a kiss on the forehead.

"Sleep tight, old woman," I said. "I'll see you tomorrow."

The kids made breakfast the next morning, and as I was putting on my coat, the phone rang. It was the caregiver at Edith's house.

"I think you need to come right now," she said, evenly and calmly but with a persistence that let me know this was a serious moment. "She's not doing very well."

She asked me if she should call the aid unit.

It didn't take me long to reach a decision.

"No," I said. "You just sit tight. I've already got my coat on. I'll be right there."

I had prepared for this moment. I knew there was no sense in prolonging things just for the sake of prolonging them. Another week like this wouldn't mean anything. I'd talked to Edith about it as well: She was a little more reluctant to talk about it than I thought she'd be, but she faced the questions about as bravely as you can expect anyone to. I had the documentation plastered all over her house—the do-not-resuscitate order and all.

It took me about forty minutes to drive to Edith's. Part of me knew this moment was coming. But only part of me. I was ready. And I wasn't ready. I wanted it to be over. I didn't want it to be over. I sped up. I slowed down. I picked up my cell phone. I put it down. I gripped the wheel tighter. I made myself relax.

She's gone.

She isn't gone.

It's time.

It isn't time.

I've said all I can say.

There's so much more to say.

There's nothing more to say.

• • •

The caregiver was waiting for me when I walked in the door. I could tell by the look on her face. I walked over to Edith and picked up her hand, and held it in mine for a moment, and then placed it gently down on her lap. I felt for her pulse, but I didn't really need to do that. I knew that it was over.

I called the hospice people, and then I just sat quietly with Edith until they arrived.

They showed up quickly, and were just as sweet and calm as they'd been all along. We talked about a lot of mundane details—they'd take care of sending back the wheelchair, the leftover meds, they'd handle all of that.

A van showed up from the funeral home, and they placed Edith on a gurney. I took her hand one more time, and bent over and kissed her forehead one more time.

One last time.

They wheeled her out to the van, but I stayed behind in the house. I realized I'd been terrified that there would be a big media circus around this moment, that I'd have to deal with all those reporters and their questions, but it was calm and perfectly quiet.

I couldn't bring myself to sit down on the couch, but just stood and stared at it. Edith's mother had died on this very couch, I thought. And all Edith wanted in life was to die on this couch as well. And now she had.

I had promised to do a thing. And now the thing was done.

And now what?

Now what?

The question just sat there, on the couch, where Edith

had been. The sun was high in the sky outside now, and it was glinting off those gold etchings on the wall.

I started thinking about all those stories: Lionel Barrymore. Benny Goodman. Richard Tauber. Hitler. Mickey Rooney.

It suddenly struck me as funny: I bet that's the first time anyone ever said those two names together. Hitler and Mickey Rooney.

I laughed for just a second. And then, finally, the tears that had been waiting, patiently, as my efficient do-what-needs-to-be-done self did what he needed to do, the tears that had been respectfully waiting in the corner, came like a storm, and I did nothing to try to hold them back.

Those stories. Whether they were true, or whether she made them up, they had sustained me, all those months, all those long nights, they were there, in the room, and now they were gone. The stories, those mysterious and wonderful stories, were over.

17

I tried to go to work the next day, but I couldn't. I just went into Edith's house, and sat in the living room chair opposite the couch, and stared out the window. I spent the morning thinking about how everything looked exactly the same—the TV, the movies, the books, the sheets on the couch, the water and the pills and the tissue box still waiting for Edith on the coffee table, the papers piled up on her desk, the little miniature ceramic animals on the windowsill—everything was the same. And nothing was the same.

About an hour after I got there, I got a phone call from my buddy Clayton that I used to work with, and he was telling me he was sorry that she'd passed.

"Well, how do you know that?" I asked.

"I heard it on the radio," he said, "when I was coming to work."

I almost felt their presence before I saw them. I turned around, and looked out the window, and there they all were, the newspaper reporters and the TV crews, all camped out on the sidewalk. It wasn't like the movies at all—they weren't all rowdy and full of themselves, just a bunch of young people standing around and waiting. Waiting for me, though, which made it pretty strange.

I couldn't even begin to think about talking to them. I just hid out in the house all day, kind of like a lost dog, wandering around and not knowing what to do or where to go. I kept thinking of things I needed to do for Edith—prescriptions to fill, food to buy, dishes to clean—and then a second later I realized, well, no, I guess I don't need to do those things anymore. Each time, it was like Edith was leaving me again, and each time, I'd start to tear up once more.

The reporters finally gave up and went home, and a little while later so did I. It's kind of a blur, but I did talk to them at some point, maybe the next day or the day after that. Somewhere along the line they had stopped casting me as the evil developer. Now I was the best thing since sliced bread to them, and they were pretty respectful. I thought it was odd that through the whole process, none of them ever showed up at my home. It's not like I'm that hard to find. But maybe that was out of respect, too, and I guess I'm very thankful to them for all that. I especially felt it in those days, those first days, as I was getting ready for Edith's funeral.

The Tuesday after she died I went back to the house to meet Edith's friend Gail, and we spent about a half-day picking out what clothes Edith would wear, and what perfume, and such. I just couldn't decide; it seemed so terribly important. Edith, for all her bluster, was always someone who cared about what she looked like, who cared about appearances, who cared about what other people thought. The same woman who could tell CBS News to go to hell would never leave the house in a scarf that didn't match her sweater.

We took the stuff down to the funeral home. I was bracing myself to talk about the funeral arrangements, but the man I met there, a skinny fellow in an old black suit, told me that Edith had already taken care of everything, which kind of surprised me. I knew what Edith wanted. She didn't want a ceremony, she just wanted to be put in a simple box, and buried in a double-stacker grave, on top of her mother. "It'll be the first time with my mother," I remember her telling me, "that I ever wound up on top." But I didn't know she'd contacted the funeral home and got everything set up—and had done so nearly fifteen years ago.

She had also told them that she wanted to be buried right away. So a few days later, when we held her ceremony, Edith was already in the ground.

She'd picked the music for her service, some quiet classical music, and it was playing when we showed up at the funeral home. The service was held in a little mini-chapel, just a small room with an altar and a couple dozen folding chairs. I had called some people who knew Edith or who'd helped her out over the years, but I'd made a point of keeping it quiet as far as the media were concerned. I sure didn't need that circus on this day. We all sat quietly for a while, and just as the ceremony was about to start, I heard a noise behind me, and turned around.

It was Charlie.

I had called and left a message for him the day Edith died; he never called me back, so I didn't know if he was even going to show up. He looked like hell, to tell you the truth. His shirt looked like it had been rolled up in a big ball in the trunk of his car or something. He himself looked like he had just rolled out of bed and hadn't bothered to comb his hair. I guess you have to give him credit for driving all the way down, and I guess I was kinda glad he came. Something in his manner told me he was still pissed off at me. But I didn't really care about that one way or the other.

When I was going through Edith's clothes, I noticed all the little gold crosses on the lapels, and I took them all off to give them to Edith's friends. I also happened across a green necklace and earring set; it was her birthstone. I thought it was emeralds, but Evie told me it was something called peridot. Charlie's wife was also born in August, so it would have been her birthstone as well. Edith wanted me to have everything else, but she once said she wanted Charlie's wife to have those, so I made a point of bringing them to the service in case he showed up. I shook his hand, and gave him the jewelry, and let him choose which of the crosses he wanted. And then I turned away.

It was a simple service. They'd asked me if I wanted to speak, but of course I couldn't. I could barely go five minutes without starting to cry; there was no way I could have made it through two sentences up there. But I was glad we had the service, just to give everybody that moment. That chance to say good-bye.

It wasn't that moment, for me. I couldn't even begin to

think about saying good-bye to Edith, and I wouldn't be able to for a long time. I was just trying to get through the day without making a fool of myself.

I was itching to get back to Edith's house, for some reason. I just felt I needed to be there. Maybe it was like I wanted to go back to check, to see if it was all just some big mistake, and that she'd still be on the couch. "Well, where the hell have *you* been all day?" she'd yell at me.

"I had to go to your funeral," I'd say to her.

"Well, don't be in such a big hurry," she'd say. "I can't go just yet. You can't do anything by yourself. You still have too much to learn."

The day after Edith died happened to be the day we were taking the crane down; I had been secretly glad it was going to be such a busy day, because it kept my mind off of things as much as possible. But of course, that only went so far.

In the days, and weeks, that followed, I'd go over to Edith's house in the afternoons, with the intention of trying to figure out what to do with her stuff. I knew that my inability to move anything was silly, but there it was. I'd bring out a garbage bag and walk around aimlessly, picking things up and putting them down, and wind up a half-hour later with an empty bag. Or I'd bring a cardboard box to gather things I could give away to charity, and walk back to my trailer with the box still empty.

Late one afternoon, as I walked over to Edith's, I noticed that things seemed particularly quiet. I don't know what it was. Some days just seem like that, in the early summer, when the air is getting hotter and heavier and maybe sound doesn't travel so well, but the background noise of life—the compressors and generators from the construction site, the rumble of complaining engines grinding their way up the slope of the bridge to Seattle—all seemed kind of far away. It makes you feel a little lost in your thoughts, a little lonely, I guess. Maybe I was just missing Edith more that day. I let out a big sigh as I went into her house. As usual, I just wandered around for a while, not really knowing what I was doing there or what I wanted to be doing there. I sat down at her desk to survey all the paper I knew I'd eventually have to make some accounting of. There were her books, the ones she always wanted to have published. I felt guilty that I'd never read them, but I don't think Edith ever expected me to. She knew I wasn't much of a reader, and I know she wouldn't have given a good goddamn what I thought about them, but I guess I felt like I should have picked one of them up at some point. I kept meaning to, but something always kept me from it.

I made my way up to the attic, which was through a door off her bedroom, to try to sort through some of what she had stored up there, and noticed something I had never noticed before. There were two small books tucked away on the far shelf. One was about four inches square, with a cloth cover, kind of a sea-foam green; the word *Autographs* was embossed on the front. The other was an eight-by-eleven book with a hard leather cover, black, with a kind of scrolling detail in gray. Very old and very fancy.

I opened the bigger one first, and the first page I opened to gave me a start. Staring back at me was a pencil sketch—not all that professional, more like something you'd see a high school art student do, but still pretty realistic. And written in script on the bottom left side it said, "Marlene Dietrich." On the next page, another sketch, and I didn't have to look at the legend to realize it was Spencer Tracy.

Well, that old wack job, I said to myself. She actually sat around drawing pictures of these people. That's how real they were to her.

I saw that a bunch of the pages were signed with autographs. I read the first one: "Dear Edith, I have such a nice memory of you always. I hope you have too, your cousin Irving Goodman."

Well, that wasn't so surprising. I guess I always knew that Benny Goodman really was her cousin. I guess he must have had a brother named Irving.

But when I put that book down and opened the smaller one, I couldn't believe what I was looking at.

Written in pen, in a very old-fashioned script, it said,

Dear Edith,
When you're rich have lots of dough
send gifts to your friends I know
so when you pass out gifts don't miss
just send out Clark a great big kiss.
                    Yours, Clark Gable

I knew Edith's handwriting, and this wasn't it. Could it actually be—could Clark Gable have actually written that to her? It was like finding the key to a door that's been locked for years. It opened so easily.

I looked at the next page. In writing that was not at all similar to the previous page, it read:

> *July 8, 1942*
> *Dear Edith,*
> *There is nothing more I could wish for thee*
> *but health happiness and prosperity.*
> *Your friend, Katharine Hepburn*

I stared at it for the longest time. These are not things that celebrities write when you shove an autograph book under their noses. These are things people write to old friends.

I kind of sleepwalked down the stairs to the chair opposite the couch, and sat down, so I could look at the book in a better light. The afternoon was hazy, and gave everything a kind of gauzy glow. Or maybe it was my state of mind that made it seem like that. But page after page, the past came rushing into that room—or I was being drawn into the past— like somebody'd opened up a portal in an old sci-fi movie. I felt like I could see back through time. And I was just slack-jawed at what I was seeing. One after another, the celebrities of another time pledged their love and devotion to their dear friend.

Their dear friend Edith Macefield.

March 1937

Dear Edith,

I'll put my thought way down in here
tucked away beneath the pages
and then I know that you will call me
On down through the ages.

> *As always, Spencer Tracy*

Edith,
I hope you will always be successful and happy
as you have been a real friend to me.

> *George Raft*

Dear Edith,
Thanks for the wonderful long years of friendship you have
given me, you may not remember but I can never forget.

> *Your sincere friend, Jimmy Dorsey*

It went on and on: Tommy Dorsey, Chicago 1943. Pau-
lette Goddard. Julie Dorsey.

And this:

New York, 1941
I have enjoyed you with the band, wish
you the best of success in the future.

> *Guy Lombardo*

Holy shit! She sang—or played clarinet, or something—
with Guy Lombardo's band, and never got around to mentioning it? Is that possible?

Ma petite Cherie,
I hope that when you think of me
you'll also think of Gay Paris.

                    Merci beaucoup, Maurice Chevalier

I kept flipping the pages, and each was more unbelievable than the one before. Josephine Baker writes, "I wish you years of great success and then I wish you all the rest." Here's Victor Lombardo, Skip Dorsey, Gregory Peck, Woody Herman. Irene Dunne. Doris Day.

Errol Flynn.

The dates ranged all through the war years, and after. Jean Harlow writes in 1937, Charlie Chaplin—Charlie goddamn Chaplin! writes in 1941. And look at this one:

Dear Edith,
You can sing to a rat
you can sing to a mouse
but I'd rather you sing
to Johann Strauss.

                    Ronald Colman

I picked up the first book again, and I don't know how long I sat there staring at the sketches. The Marlene Dietrich one, with those glaring eyes. Will Rogers.

I looked in the back of the book, and I saw that the later sketches were signed, and I compared those signatures with the ones under the little poems in the other book, and they matched.

And all I could think was, well, *la-di-friggin-da*.

She was telling the truth, all that time.

I got up and looked out the window. The light was starting to dim now. I must have been sitting there for an hour, I thought. I looked up at the clock, and realized I'd better get on the road and head home. I had been coming home for dinner at a normal time since Edith died and nobody had said anything, but I knew Evie and the kids appreciated it. I wanted to bring that book home to show Evie, but I still couldn't bring myself to take anything out of the house just yet.

I sat down on the living room chair one more time, and looked over at the couch where Edith always sat. I still hadn't moved anything, the pillows or the sheets. I could still sense her presence, the feel of her. I could imagine what her skin looked like, her face, the tremble in her hand as she reached for a glass of water, the way the water would ripple in the glass as she pulled it toward her.

I tried to understand why she never showed me that book, and the more I thought about it, the more sense it made. This was a woman who never felt like she had to explain herself or justify herself. She did what she wanted to do because she wanted to do it, and because she thought it was the right thing. She moved back here to take care of her mother because that's what you do, in the same way I spent all those days and nights here taking care of her, because that's just what you do. She stayed here because she wanted to, because this is where she felt she belonged, and as much as the world wanted to pester her with questions about why she turned down a million dollars, she never felt like she owed them an explanation.

As close as Edith and I became, she never owed me an explanation for anything, either. But it went beyond that: I think it was almost like showing me the book would be like admitting she needed my approval. Like it mattered to her whether or not I believed her. And that's just not Edith. She had no reason to ever think I would doubt the stories she told—and screw you, Barry Martin, if you don't believe them. She couldn't give a rat's ass about what I thought.

And it was more than that, too. The past was a living, breathing thing for Edith, one that she had left behind her; it had its wonders, but it was always threatening, in some way, to swallow her up if she allowed it. And she wasn't the kind of woman who would let yesterday drag her down.

And yet, that autograph book. That autograph book, I realized, was a document, a testament, to the place where that yesterday began.

Where yesterday began? I thought. I couldn't place, for a second, where that phrase had come from. And then I remembered.

I walked back over to the little table next to Edith's desk, the one that the big doorstop of a book lived on. I looked at the cover.

Where Yesterday Began.

I picked it up. It was even heavier than it looked. I tucked it under my arm, and without thinking about it much, opened the front door and walked out, locking the door behind me, and headed for my car.

18

It was just after Labor Day when I got the call that my mom was in the hospital. She had had a stroke.

They had taken her in an ambulance to Shelton General, the hospital closest to their house. My dad had long since accepted that he's not allowed to drive anymore, and even as the Alzheimer's got worse he seemed to remember that, but the first thing I did was to call him and tell him I'd come get him, and not to drive to the hospital. It took me about an hour and a half to get down to him, and then I turned around and we went to the hospital together. When I got there, I was stunned to find out that they were getting ready to discharge my mom.

Or they thought they were, anyway.

The nurse told me that my mom had just had what they called a "mini-stroke." But the more I questioned her, and the more I didn't get answers, the more I realized that the nurse didn't know thing one about what was going on. Someone had handed her a chart and said this patient is being discharged, and so in her mind this was a person who didn't need to be in the hospital anymore, and that was that.

But that, I informed her, was nowhere near close to that.

I was just being obstinate for the sake of being obstinate, at that point, because I knew it was just a matter of minutes before she told me to wait one moment and she would get the doctor. Sure enough, that's what happened.

I also knew from past experience that one moment was going to be a lot more than one moment, so I went back in to see Mom. She seemed to be doing pretty well. She's stoic, by nature, so I think she could have gotten hit by a Mack truck and say she was doing fine, but it was still reassuring to see her so chipper, considering. Finally, the doctor showed up. A nice fellow, about ten years younger than me, but a lot taller. I came up to about the shoulder of his white coat.

I started asking lots of very specific questions: What happened to my mother? Why were they discharging her so soon? What should we expect? What should we be watching for? Will there be any signs that will tell us if it's something worse than you think? What caused this? How should we follow up? Are there any other tests that can be done, or is this only a wait-and-see situation?

The doctor wasn't fazed at all by my attitude. Quite the contrary: I got the sense that he actually liked it when family members took an active involvement. He patiently answered all my questions, and told me about all the tests that had been done. He said we could wait here for the blood work to come back if we wanted, but unless it showed something they didn't expect, there was no real reason to remain. The most important thing was to get her back in her own comfortable environment where she could rest. He told me that the blood work would let them know if any additional medications were needed, but at the moment the recommended treatment was to give her aspirin to thin her blood, and watch for any symptoms—numbness, tingling, blurred vision, slurred speech—that could indicate another stroke. I felt better after talking to him, and we got ready to help bring my mom home.

I think the whole experience, though, brought my parents more to my attention. As much as they were understanding of all the time I'd spent with Edith, I still had missed a lot of time with them over the last two years. I went to visit more often in the weeks after my mom got home from the hospital. On one of those visits, I wandered into the living room, where my dad was on the couch, juice in hand, watching a *Bonanza* rerun.

Then and there, I made a decision. My mom would be dead set against it at first, but another thing I'd learned from dealing with a stubborn bulldog of an old lady is that I could be pretty stubborn myself.

And this was something I needed to do. It would take me a while to get around to it, but I had it set in my mind, and knew that I probably couldn't put it off too long. Come next spring, or early summer at the latest, we had to do it, and I wasn't going to take no for an answer.

It was time for me and my dad to go fishing.

• • •

It was the next spring, May 2009, when I was finally finishing up the mall. We had a little problem getting the last two elevators, two big fancy ones from Schindler, one of the biggest elevator companies in the world, but they finally arrived, and I could sense the finish line. Edith's house was still sitting there, right in the middle of this big shopping mall. She had left me the house in her will, and told me to sell it to pay for my kids' education, but so far I couldn't bring myself to do anything about it. She was insistent on one thing: "Get your price for it," she told me over and over. It was important to her.

The developers had waited a respectable amount of time before even asking me what I was going to do with the house, which is a good thing, because if they had pushed me in those first few months, I probably would have decked them. It was just too emotional. But finally we started talking about it, and they made an offer—not the price I wanted, but a halfway decent figure. We were supposed to get together and seal the deal, and we set a meeting for eleven o'clock one Monday morning early in May, at the mall.

When I pulled up, I kept noticing, in a way I had never really noticed before, how small Edith's house seemed, sitting there in the middle of the project. You know, when you see something all day long, every day, it doesn't seem strange to you after a while. And after Edith's death, I was so wrought up, I couldn't think of anything, really. But now I had to decide what I was going to do with that silly little house, closed in on three sides by a bright, shiny new shopping mall.

When eleven o'clock rolled around, the developers still hadn't shown up. I was hanging out in the office, chatting with my foreman, Kent, when my cell phone rang. Had the developers been on time, I probably wouldn't have picked up, and everything that was about to happen wouldn't have happened. But having nothing else to do but wait, I took the call.

Just by coincidence—or maybe not—the call was from a guy I had talked to once or twice, who was interested in the property. He told me how much he would pay for Edith's house, and it was more than the developers were offering. I told him about the meeting with the developers, and how that was kind of a done deal. He said nothing's done until it's done.

I was really feeling torn. Did I owe it to the developers to sell them the place? Did I owe it to Edith not to? Did I owe it to my kids to just get the best price I could?

It was about 11:20 when I hung up the phone. Now I was really flummoxed about what to do. Kent and I found ourselves wandering around the area across the street from the mall project, where they had demolished some buildings for new offices that still haven't gone up. I stood there for a moment, looking back at the project. There was Edith's house, squatting in its little space like a cat in the middle of a gigantic sofa. It didn't look like it was going anywhere. You couldn't imagine the mall closing in on it, swallowing it up. I couldn't imagine the house going away—and yet I couldn't imagine for the life of me why someone would want to buy it and live there. On the other hand, there really was something to that house. It was an oddity, but one way or the other it was my oddity now, and it was filled with Edith's spirit.

I still thought about her every day. About our routines,

about having someone to spend the day with who needed you so thoroughly, and about the feeling of making a promise and keeping it. But more than anything else, I thought about her stories. Ever since I'd found that autograph book, those stories had come alive for me. It was hard to believe that I would never hear any more of them. That I would never hear her voice again.

And suddenly—I don't even know how to say this, but I promise that this is true. Because I wasn't the only one who heard it.

From somewhere above me, a woman's voice yelled, "Barry!"

I looked around. We were all alone. There was a long pause, and then for a second time, I heard it again: "Barry!"

I surveyed the area again. There was no one up on the sidewalk. There was no one back on the bridge. I looked at Kent—and he was swiveling around, looking around as well.

"Kent," I said, almost in a whisper, "did you hear that? Did someone call my name?"

"Someone called your name," he said. "Twice."

When he said that, I about fell over. I got a chilly feeling in my arms and the back of my legs. I kept looking around, but there was no one there. I asked Kent where he thought the voice came from.

Kent pointed to the sky.

"It came from there, Barry," he said. "It was Edith."

Make of it what you will. Believe it if you want, or don't. All I know is I'd spent my whole life believing that there's nothing after you die, that you go to the dirt and that's the end of it. We're alone down here, and when we're done down here, we're done.

I don't believe that anymore.

By the time the developers showed up, I'd had time to think about this guy's offer. To be honest, I don't think the developers still had their heart in this fight. The mall was done—it had an odd little shape to it, working its way around that little house, but it was done; I don't know how much they cared about taking the walls down and picking up those few extra square feet anymore. The other fellow was offering me a lot more money. And maybe there was something about Edith's presence that morning that guided me, or maybe not.

I decided, ultimately, to go with the other fellow's deal. And later, when I found out what he wanted it for, I was really, really glad I did.

19

The one thing I had promised myself, and had followed through on, was the decision to take my dad on a fishing trip. I had gotten an e-mail from this website I look at all the time, and it talked about a trip up to Alaska, so I clicked on the link and checked it out and thought, wow, that would just be a lot of fun. It was on the Nushagak River. You can get all the Pacific salmon up there—king, coho, sockeye, chum. The best are the king salmon, which run from about the middle of June to the middle of July. The place I decided we'd stay was a lodge called King Salmon, in fact. I talked to Willy, who had just finished his first year at the community college, and told him I thought it would be great if he came with us, and I didn't have to ask him twice.

I talked to my dad, and his first reaction was, "Your mother would never go for it." He was right about that one. But there's a story he always told about a survey ship he was once on in Alaska, and he always ended that story—the way parents always repeat themselves when they tell stories, even when they don't have Alzheimer's—saying, "I'd love to go back up there one day."

So I said, "Dad, just tell me, do you want to go?"

"Sure I do," he said.

"Well then, I'm gonna make it happen."

My mom, as expected, was dead set against it. She kept reminding me of how he'd wandered off down the trail under the power lines. If we can't keep track of him right there at home, she kept saying, how the heck are you going to take care of him when he's got all of Alaska to wander off in? He can't even put on his shoes by himself. How are you going to manage?

I just stuck to my guns and told her that I could take care of him, and that Willy would be there to help me. I'm not sure why I was so gung-ho about this trip. I guess I wanted us to all have one big, lasting memory. But on top of that, I just didn't want to see my dad sitting around all day. I think that's another tendency we have, when people get sick. We want them to just sit in a dark room, quietly, and preserve their energy and strength, and keep them out of trouble. That's just fine for some; for others it's a death sentence, a way of pulling pages off the calendar until you get to the one with the big black mark on it. My dad was always such an active guy, so interested in things, and he loved the water so much. I remembered him steering that boat, a million years ago, and the look on his face when he was out on the water— and I could imagine the look on my face as I admired him— and I thought he deserved at least one more moment like that. To be honest, I was kind of nervous about the whole thing—I mean, my mother did have a point—but I wasn't going to let anyone know that.

When I finished off the elevators in the mall, that was my last day on the job. I was lucky enough to have another one lined up, so I didn't even take a day off in between. You'd think you'd have a big celebration when a job like building a mall is completed, but work is work, and the very next day I was down south in Milton, where I'd been asked to take over a large project. It was an assisted-living facility sitting on 23 acres. Once again, I was struck by the irony of the situation; of being asked to build one, after two years of trying to keep an old lady out of them.

We had scheduled the fishing trip for the end of June. A few weeks before we left, I was talking to one of the painters on the new job. It somehow came out that we were both fishermen—no big surprise when you get a couple of Washington boys together—but when I mentioned to him that in a month and a half I was headed up to the Nushagak, his eyebrows kind of went up. "Really? Where are you staying?" he asked me.

I told him we were going to the King Salmon, and his eyebrows went up again.

"No kidding," he said. "I used to own that."

Turns out he and a couple of his partners had just sold the place. This was the first year he wasn't going up in as long as he could remember. They had a deal to run the place for two more years. "One of my partners is up there right now," he told me.

I couldn't believe my luck. I explained about my dad, and

told the painter that I was bringing him along, but I was a little nervous because he had Alzheimer's, and I could probably use a little help in watching out for him.

The guy made sure his partners up in Alaska knew who we were, so before we even set foot on Alaskan soil, they were ready to lend a hand.

It was such a lucky turn of events; before my whole experience with Edith, I would have just sloughed it off as a coincidence, but now I wasn't so sure. I felt, deep in my bones, that somebody up there was watching out for me.

If you know what I mean.

Mom brought my dad over on Sunday around noon, so we could get all our stuff together and consolidate our gear. He showed up with two army duffel bags, one with his clothes all packed, the other pretty much empty, for hauling our gear. I saw him standing there in the doorway, wearing a pair of sweats, a green knit shirt, and a baseball cap. Not to mention the biggest grin on his face I'd seen in years. He was just raring to go.

We got up at oh-dark-thirty the next morning. Dad managed to dress himself, although I had to help him get his belt through the loops, and we all piled into my Ford F-350 Turbo Diesel and hit the road. It felt so right, to be with my son and my father.

I had had a talk with Willy, that one of us had to keep an eye on Grandpa at all times. Willy understood that my dad was having issues—we'd been pretty open and honest with him—and seemed ready to step up and help. We all wanted this to be a great memory, and Willy understood that he had to play his part to make that happen.

Dad sat by the window on the first flight, up to Anchorage, and he was like a little kid, commenting on everything as the scenery slow-dissolved to the mountains and glaciers of Alaska. "Willy, look at that volcano down there," he said, patting Willy on the arm. "Is that something or is that something?"

We had a short layover in Anchorage, which was something of a trip in and of itself, because they've got these big glass cases with stuffed grizzlies and polar bears and wolves—most of them are world record animals, so you can get kind of lost gawking at the stuff. And sure enough, I went to the bathroom, and when I came out I found Willy staring up at a big Kodiak bear—and no sign of Dad.

I panicked, and started running down the hall. A little ways along I found my father. He had a strange look on his face, like he wasn't quite sure what was going on. I started to get angry, but then I took a moment to catch my breath. In that moment I saw him, walking slowly, alone, and I tried to imagine the world from his point of view—how it was turning and twisting a little, like a Rubik's cube, and he was just having trouble keeping up with it. It made me sad, but it also made me proud, how well he was hanging on, how game he was to take this trip.

"Hey, Dad," I finally said to him, "What's going on?"

"Oh, nothing," he said. "You know the life span of these Kodiaks isn't much more than a dog's, isn't that something?"

I steered him back over to our gate, and found Willy. Out of Dad's earshot I reminded him that one of us had to keep an eye on him at every second. You don't have to hold him down, you just have to know where he's headed. Willy was very apologetic, but I told him that we were lucky it had happened now, to help us remember what we had to do. That seemed to go down well with him.

Our next flight got us up to Dillingham, just about an hour and a half's flight, and one of the most beautiful you could ever take. I looked out the window, and saw the tundra and the rivers. The land is so flat that the waters just meander; some of the switchbacks aren't more than a hundred yards apart. If you're looking for a place that will make you turn off your sense of always trying to move forward in one direction, this is about as good as any.

In Dillingham, we caught a little twelve-seat float plane, and pretty soon we were flying over the camp. You could see that it was basically a collection of little canvas Quonset huts. We landed right on the river, and they sent little boats out to get us. Friendly folks, and solid—you felt secure right away when you met these people, they so clearly knew what they were doing. Sure enough, one of the fellows noticed that my dad was moving kind of slow; I don't know if he'd already been alerted that we were coming today (or, if he had, that he had figured out Dad was the one my painter friend had called about), but he made a beeline for my dad and offered him a ride up the hill in a little six-wheel dune buggy they had for running around the camp. I was already starting to feel more assured—but oddly, it wasn't like they were tamping down some great fear I had. Even though I was way off in the Alaskan wilderness with a man capable of wandering off at the sight of a stuffed bear, I had the strongest sense that I really, really could handle this. I know I kept telling my mom that, to calm her down—but I didn't have to keep telling myself that. Somehow, I knew it already.

They took us up to show us the cabins, and it was basically two people to a cabin, so my dad and I grabbed one and Willy grabbed another with a fellow we'd met on the plane. The cabins were all named after different kinds of salmon; ours was Chinook.

They showed us how to fire up the propane heater in our hut; it wasn't that cold, considering, but our guide said, "Trust me, you'll need this. It can get pretty chilly at night."

It was getting on to lunchtime, so they took us up to the main cabin, gave us some lunch, and assigned us our guide. Finally, it was time to get in some fishing.

Dad had trouble working the reel, which was hard for me to see because it was something he'd been doing his whole life. Not that his hands wouldn't work, more like he just couldn't figure out how to operate the thing. I resisted the urge to grab it out of his hands and do it for him.

We were fishing maybe five minutes when Willy got the first salmon. Big one, too. A few minutes later, Dad got one on the line. I could tell he was struggling with it—he didn't have his sea legs, and with the arthritis it was hard for him to grip the rod. He seemed a little confused, too. At one point, the fish was running and Dad got his hands in the way of the line, and the line was going across his hand and I knew it would cut him, so this time I did grab the reel from him for a moment to get him right. He didn't seem too upset about it, just kind of confused, but I didn't make a big deal about it. Once I got the fish a little closer in, I gave the rod back to him and let him finish it off, but I was thinking, man, this is going to be a long trip.

But the second fish he got on the line, well, that was my dad, all the way. He jumped right up, and I could see that he had it under control, like it was ten years ago. Like it was fifty years ago. I looked over at Willy, and for a second it was me who had just graduated high school, and I'm watching my dad, the pro, the master, bring in a king salmon, and all is right with the world.

You need four to fill a boat, in addition to the guide, so along with me, Dad, and Willy, there was Helmut, a nice guy who owned a glass company. He spoke German; his English was broken but good enough that we could figure each other out. It was another amazing coincidence—remember those two Schindler elevators we were waiting on to finish the mall project? They were glass elevators, and it turns out that the glass for those elevators came from Helmut's company. And here I run into him next to me in a boat in the middle of Alaska. Go figure.

Helmut may have run a good company, but he couldn't catch a fish to save his life. Nice enough fellow to have in the boat, though. Generally, when you go out, there's one side of the boat where the fishing's better. Or seems to be, anyway. So for the first couple of days, we're banging 'em one after another, and Helmut's just sitting there with his pole in the water, looking kind of wistful. These salmon are running like 25 or 30 pounds, and the days are going by and Helmut hasn't had a chance to fight one of them. So the third or fourth time this happens, we switch Helmut over to the side where everybody's catching salmon—and, wouldn't you know it, suddenly he's on the cold side again, with us sitting where he'd been, still banging 'em one after another. Sometimes, fishing will break your heart just because it can.

We were scheduled to be there for six days; it never really gets dark, that far north at that time of the year, it just kind of hits twilight and stays that way. You get a little fouled up because you're not quite sure when to go to sleep, and to tell you the truth I could have fished twenty-four hours a day for six days and not known the difference. But like with anything else, you get into a kind of routine, you have breakfast, go out in the morning, back for lunch, and then out again. Dad handled it pretty well, the first day or two. There were some moments—like the first morning, when we got up, and I looked over, and Dad had his shirt on upside down and backwards.

I didn't make a big deal of it, I didn't get upset, and I certainly didn't go over and dress my father like he was a two-year-old. I just tried to make light of it, and Dad chuckled when I pointed it out. I showed him how to get himself straightened out, and then walked out of the tent and gave him a minute to get the shirt on correctly by himself. When I came in, he was all fixed up. I knew that everything wasn't perfect, but I also knew that for the most part, Dad was handling this trip okay.

But on the third day, we were coming out after lunch, and there's a little set of six or eight stairs going out from the deck down to the ground. Dad was fussing with his glasses as he was walking, and he can't really multitask anymore, and sure enough—I saw it coming a split second before it happened, but couldn't react fast enough—boom, down he goes, rolling down the stairs and onto the ground.

Oh, God, I thought. Here we go.

A couple of guys came running over, and I ran over, and Dad was on the ground, and before anyone could say anything—I could see the panic in their eyes—I spoke first, making light of the moment as much as I could, given that my heart was about in my throat.

"Hey, Dad, what the heck are you doing?"

"Oh, I'm okay," he says. "You know, this was part of being a paratrooper. They teach you how to fall. Did you see that tuck and roll? That's what I've been trying to teach you. About time you saw somebody do it right."

Sure enough, once you thought about it, he had fallen perfectly—a movie stuntman couldn't have done it better. The people who'd gathered around smiled at each other—you could see them all kind of take a collective deep breath—and they helped Dad to his feet.

"I think I'll head back down to our unit," Dad said. I told him I'd be right behind him. I ducked back into the main cabin to use the bathroom, then double-timed back to our cabin. He wasn't there, so I figured he'd stopped next door at Willy's unit.

He wasn't there, either.

I was kicking myself—I couldn't believe I'd let him out of my sight. I guess after he came through that fall so well, I just wanted to believe he was perfectly capable of taking care of himself for a few minutes. You think there are moments of lucidity and moments of confusion, and there are, but the lines between those states aren't clear. They come and go in a second and you have to be there to notice the change.

And I wasn't there.

I ran down to the riverbank, and then back to Willy's. "Willy, we've got to go find Grandpa. I don't know where the hell he's at."

He threw his boots on and we ran out. I was afraid Dad would get lost in the woods behind the camp, so we headed in that direction. I was thankful that it was never going to get dark, but that was about all I was thankful for.

We were passing the last of the Quonset huts when the door swung open. And there, walking slowly out into the fading light, was Dad.

"What the heck—" I heard my voice, angry and frustrated, and took a breath and started again. "Hey, what the heck are you doing in there, Dad?"

"Well, I'm not really sure," he said.

I was shaking, literally, from the adrenaline draining out of my arms and legs. I put my arm around Dad's shoulder and headed him back toward our cabin. "We're over here, in Chinook, Dad," I said. "Remember Chinook."

"Chinook," he said, his voice childlike and quiet. I think he understood that he'd gotten lost; I think he maybe even understood that, unlike the previous times, somebody was covering for him—no one was going to yell at him like a child. I hoped, somewhere deep down, that he got that. And that he appreciated it. I think it meant a lot to him.

I hope it did. In the end we are old-school men. We are not going to sit around a circle and talk about our feelings and link arms and sing "Kumbaya." We just do what we have to do. I wasn't about to ask him what was going through his mind, or his heart, any more than he was about to ask me the same. I just walked him back to our cabin, and we sat down and talked about fish; who had caught what that day, and what we thought we might go after tomorrow.

Willy wandered by, and I pulled him outside the cabin, and made sure he knew this wasn't his fault, that it was all mine, but that we needed to double down on keeping track of Grandpa. We had gotten away with this twice—once in the airport and once today—so we really shouldn't test the theory that the third time's the charm.

The lessons I learned from Edith came back, again and again, as I went through the week with my dad. The next night, Dad was eating a bowl of shrimp and asked me if I'd get him a cup of coffee. I said I would, but must have gotten distracted, because the next thing I knew he had walked over to the coffee urn and carefully poured coffee directly into his bowl of shrimp. Once again, I started to react badly—the "What the heck are you doing!" and "Why don't you just wait for me to do that for you!" rose up in me—but I just took a deep breath.

I sidled up to my father and asked, "Whatcha got goin' on there, Dad?"

He looked down at his plate and seemed confused. "I don't exactly know," he said, a little sadly.

"Can I give you a hand with that?" I asked.

"No, I can take care of it," he said.

I wasn't at all sure that he could—but I was sure that it was his decision. "Okay, I'll be over there if you need me," I said, and walked away. I tried not to let him see me watching his every move; but somehow he managed to get himself a new plate of shrimp, and a new cup of coffee, and keep them separate. He was struggling with it, but it was his struggle.

That's what I brought to the trip with me, the gift that Edith had given me: the understanding that, even though it might be easier to treat him like a child, my father is not a child. He is a man with all the pride that a man of that age, and that experience, carries with him. There were moments, like when I'd be putting sunblock on my dad's face, making sure to get it on the sides of his neck and behind his ears, that I flashed back to doing that for my kids when they were little. And in those moments, I realized that yes, I was treating my father like a child just then, but this was a necessary task, and when this task was over, I had to put those feelings away, had to let him return to being a man, to the pride that his age owns, and needs, and demands, because in many ways it is the one thing that holds him in place while the world is starting to crumble and turn around him.

The last day we were there was just a half-day; we went out in the morning, but were going to leave that afternoon. We went down to a hole they call the Swallow's Nest, and put in our lines. That day we were running plugs—a plug is a little plastic thing that dives and wiggles in the water, pulling against the current. You just drop it down near the bottom, and wiggle it in the salmon's face. It drives them crazy, and they grab for it.

Well, I don't think we were out five minutes when Dad got a hit, and you could tell right away it was a big one. A huge bronze bruiser, and it was fighting like you'd called its mother a bad name.

Willy's rod went off at the same time, so the two of them were there, fighting away, and it was one of the great moments of the trip. I tried to press it into my memory, to freeze that moment and keep it, my son and my dad, side by side, wailing away at some kick-ass salmon.

I was dying to help my dad out, and forcing myself not to. For a moment, it looked like the rod was going to fly right out of his hands. I thought, If he loses this one, it'll be just terrible. He'll be so upset. Maybe I should make sure he gets it.

Or maybe not.

He was working that baby like a maestro. He got the salmon up close to the boat, and we couldn't believe it. The biggest one I'd taken all trip weighed 32.5 pounds—and this one made it look like a teener. It was easily 40 pounds if it was an ounce.

I knew he was trying not to make a big deal of it—but he was smiling so wide you'd think the top of his head would have come off at the hinges. My dad, it became apparent, had just caught the biggest fish of the trip.

Willy was going nuts—"You got it, Grandpa! That's the biggest one!" and Dad, in that old-guy way, just put his head down and said, "Well, I don't really know. Maybe so."

"Maybe so, Dad," I said. "Maybe so."

As we headed back I thought about my mom, and how she didn't want us to make the trip. How she said, well, you won't know what to expect.

And that's the truth. I certainly didn't expect this.

We headed back for the camp, with Willy still all worked up over my dad catching the biggest fish. Dad had a little grin on his face.

On the way back, we saw a big old moose swimming across the river, so we took a little detour to watch it for a while. It made shore and climbed out of the water; you couldn't tell when it was swimming, but it had to be the biggest moose in all of creation. You could probably stand and walk under it.

The boat was quiet now. We cut the motor and just sat, looking at the world around us, the woods, the water, that big elegant moose staring back at us. It was a moment, frozen in time, frozen in place, like a diorama you'd make in a shoe box for a school project when you were a kid, and for just a moment, I felt like I was outside of the shoe box, outside of the scene, looking down on it.

And just for a moment, I felt Edith's presence next to me. I hadn't thought of her much during this trip, other than noticing a hundred times over that the things I was doing with my dad, the patience I felt, all came from her. But in this moment, I did feel her presence.

I started to feel sad, but I pushed the feeling away. This

wasn't the moment for that. This was a moment to just be with my dad and my son. I just let Edith's presence be there with me, with all of us, as we sat in that moment in the sun.

After a little while the moose moved slowly away, and we headed back to camp, and got ready for the boat that would ferry us out to the seaplane.

The sun was unusually hot for Alaska, even at that time of year, so I asked Dad if I could put a little more sunscreen on him. He said sure, go ahead. And as I was rubbing it on, behind his ears and on the sides of his neck, and across the bridge of his nose, he said, "Thanks for taking care of me"; I guess he was just talking about the sunscreen, but you could kind of see in his face that maybe, in his own way, he was talking about a little more than that.

I tried to spend more time with Kelsey and Willy after I got back. It's never easy, with kids their age—there's always something they're running off to, some plan they've made that they've forgotten to tell you about. We tried instituting our family dinner again, and were pretty regular about that, but I couldn't shake the feeling that I'd lost a little something over the last year. I think every parent feels like their kids are moving away from them, a little more every day, as they get older. But I think I was feeling it more than most. I wondered whether I'd sped up that process more than I hoped to.

A while later I asked my daughter to write down some of what she was feeling about all this—I pretended it was to help me write this book, but really, if you want the truth, I wanted to hear it straight from her, in a way that I knew I could never get by talking to her face to face. She e-mailed it to me the next day, as I was driving downtown. I pulled over to look at it, and it's a good thing I did, because if I'd even glanced at it, I would have driven right off the side of the road.

I guess she couldn't decide if she was writing to me or about me—but in the end, I wouldn't change a word.

> At first when i found out that my dad was taking care of a little old lady that literally lived on your job site, I was proud, to say the least. and as the days went by my pride for my father only grew stronger. I thought that it was so cool that he was taking the little time that you had to yourself and putting it towards something that had more meaning. i have to say that when i found out about Edith for the first time i was anything but surprised. that was just like my dad to open his heart and help any and everybody in any way that he could. As time went on, i got to see more and more what my mother saw in him . . . his heart. as time went by, edith became sicker and sicker, she slowly began to lose her ability to function. Every function that she lost, was another function that my dad had to pick up.
>
> After about a year it became clear that edith was slowly deteriorating. so my father became more and more involved in everything that edith did. It was really hard on our family because my dad was always gone. he would leave for work around four in the morning and then he would get off work at around five or six at night but instead of coming home to us, he would then go to her house where he would

feed her, do her laundry, drive her to every single appointment. towards the end of this journey he even had to bathe her. she became completely dependent on him and in a ironic way he became dependent on her for her friendship. if my dad was able to come home it wasn't until 1 or 2 in the morning and then he was gone again at four. i wanted to try to lighten my father's load and i also really wanted to help edith. so i started to come and clean her house for her with my mother on weekends. we would also feed, bathe and watch over her. the thing that i missed most about having my dad around was his input. my dad will always be right there to put in his two cents and everything and let me tell you, it's a good two cents lol :) my dad committed a completely selfless act for nearly three years, that's more than most of us do in a life time. my dad stood by ediths side and guided her to her final resting place with god, and for that i am forever proud to call him my father.

    i love you dad. dont ever forget that
    your daughter

Sometimes people ask me why I did what I did.

Now they have their answer.

You do what you have to do because it's the right thing to do. And you hope that your children understand, and learn.

And there's no greater reward than finding out that, lo and behold, just when you thought they weren't paying attention to anything you said or did, it turned out that they were listening, and learning, all the time.

You don't get any luckier in life than that.

• • •

When the guy who bought Edith's house told me what he had in mind for it, I was grinning from ear to ear.

It wasn't in the contract or anything, so he could change his mind, but if he's true to his word, he's going to do something I never heard of anyone doing before.

Get this.

He told me he was going to keep Edith's house intact, but raise it up, twenty feet off the ground. He wasn't going to tie balloons to it like the little house in *Up*, but he was going to get it up there. And the space under the house he was going to enclose, to make a little public vestibule, which he was going to call Credo Square, in Edith's honor, because he felt like she lived up to her own particular credo. And for a small price, anyone who wants to can have their own personal credo etched into a tile, and that tile will be put up on the wall for all to see, from now until forever, or, as Edith would have been the first to point out, until someone takes down the mall and the house and builds some other silly thing, because that's the way of the world.

I hear the plans have changed a bit since we talked—they may not be lifting the building, at least not at first—but there's still going to be that Credo Square aspect to the thing. Which I think is nice.

I haven't decided if I'm going to put a tile up in Credo Square, or if I do, what that tile will say. Maybe I'll just say, Thanks, Edith, for all the stories. Maybe I'll crib one of those lines from her famous friends, like what Spencer Tracy wrote—

> *I'll put my thought way down in here*
> *tucked away beneath the pages*
> *and then I know that you will call me*
> *On down through the ages.*

That would be nice, because in a way, I know Edith will, indeed, keep calling on me, on down through the ages. It's a comforting thought. I loved that woman, and love her still, and in my heart I know that she loves me as well, and that nothing, not even that calendar page with the big black mark on it, can change that.

Or maybe, just for the heck of it, it'll say:

> *Dear Edith,*
> *By the living God that made you*
> *You're a better man than I am, Gunga Din!*
>> *Love, Barry*

Epilogue

A friend of mine took a read through that giant book Edith had written, *Where Yesterday Began*. She said it was an interesting story, kind of a soap opera—a long, involved tale of people falling deeply, madly in love, and all that. But it didn't seem to echo any of the stories that Edith had told me, as far as we could make out, anyway. If these were episodes from her life, then they were episodes she never shared with me, which is entirely possible.

I'd almost forgotten about a second manuscript that I found when I finally cleared out Edith's house. I almost missed it—there was a plain brown cardboard box in the bottom desk drawer, the kind of box that typing paper might have come in, before they started selling it in the shrink-wrap packages you get today. I opened it up, and saw that the top page had something typed on it. It said, in the middle of the page:

A HAZE IN AUGUST
by
DOMILINI

Domilini. The same name that Edith had used when she wrote *When Yesterday Began*. I started flipping through the pages—there were about 300 of them, all neatly typed, and from what I saw at a glance, it seemed to be another kind of soap-opera story; the couple of lines I read were very flowery and formal, and seemed to be about two people who were, guess what, deeply, madly in love.

I brought the box home and put it on a shelf in the bedroom. I meant to take it down at some point, but I guess it slipped from my memory, or, to be more honest, I just never got around to it.

But I came across it again when I was gathering some papers together to get ready to write this book, and I finally decided to just sit down and give it a read.

Holy cow.

It is the story of a young woman. A famous writer. Her name is Gennfield. She is a widow, and her dead husband's name is James, just like Edith's. The woman meets a famous performer, whom she falls in love with—but he's married, just like Richard Tauber was married, only this guy is a violinist instead of a singer.

The more I read, the more I realized: this was the story of Edith's life. I've told you more than once that I'm not much of a reader—but I went through this in one sitting. And it was like living through Edith's life, just the way she told me.

The story itself was pretty soap opera–ish, I have to say, with lots of really overwrought descriptions of this love affair (which does remain platonic, I should mention); but the details—well, they were all the details of Edith's life.

Mademoiselle Gennfield, in the book, reveals that she was a British spy as a teenager, but was captured and imprisoned in Dachau. She even describes the cell she was in. She writes about how a very powerful German, whom she had become friends with at parties in Germany before her capture, killed the guard one night and arranged her escape—the details are there, word for word, just the way Edith had told me the story. Mademoiselle Gennfield even led the children through the Alps to freedom.

Not all the children made it. There was one story Edith never told me, and when I read it here, it horrified me. I didn't know if it was true, or if she made it up for the book. Here's what she has the heroine remember:

> Karl's life blood running down a set of wide wooden steps, his fine young body all twisted and bleeding over an iron railing, the smoking luger still in the thick hand of the hard-faced German officer, the closing eyes of a tiny child melting off into death.

In the story, the woman adopts the nine surviving children. She brings them to her home, a castle of sorts, where she makes a good deal of money raising sheep.

The more I read, the more I began to wonder. Was this all real, or was this all a fantasy? Were these the stories of Edith's life, compressed into this book? Or maybe the stories Edith told me didn't really happen—maybe she wrote the book, and all these stories somehow became real to her.

The strangest thing about the story was the ending—after the love affair ends, because the guy is honorable and has to go back to his wife, the heroine starts to wonder: Did that all happen, or was it just a dream, a fantasy?

Good question, Edith. I was wondering the same thing myself.

In the end, I guess it doesn't really matter. Reading the book brought me into Edith's world, the world she lived in as a young woman. Reading her detailed descriptions of the parks and restaurants and mansions of Paris, it's like you were right there with her. Which of the details were true, and which, if any, were made up, I guess I'll never know.

I think Edith can say it a lot better than I can. This is from her prologue to the book. I didn't really get it when I read it at first, but reading it over now, I think it's maybe her final lesson for me:

> By the time I remembered this story, thirty or more years had elapsed. If a memory is too poignant, it is often consciously or unconsciously suppressed—nature's method of survival, I suppose. Nature has not, however, provided such an escape hatch for me. Those rememberings I am wont to erase, I cannot. They remain through the corridors of time as vivid as at their birthing, securely fastened in among the pleasant, the tearful, the laughing recollections.
>
> But . . . Through these many years has persisted

the sensation of having known—at some singular period—an extraordinary something that left me with a profound knowledge of unadulterated love and its incredible magic—a whisper from a long ago that hovered remotely upon the bookshelf of my mind, and flashed upon my inner eye two great lights—so profound in intensity, yet so vague in description.

The book, in the end, is about what we remember, and how we remember it. How those memories, even though they fade over time, define who we are. And I guess that's how it was with Edith and me. The memory of all that time we spent together is part of who I am now. The heroine of her story doesn't know whether the story itself is true or not. Just like I don't know what's true and what's not true in Edith's story.

But her heroine is buoyed on, through time, by the profound feelings those memories have given her.

So am I, Edith. So am I.

Acknowledgments

A few years back a young woman named Jenny Bent, who had started her own literary agency, heard about my story. Or, I should say, about Edith's story, and my part in it. She contacted me and suggested that I try to get the story down on paper—and if she hadn't done that, and a whole lot more than that, you wouldn't be holding this book right now. So I have to start by thanking her for making this happen. She heard about it from Steve Hartman, the guy who did a story on Edith for CBS. So I guess he's the one who got the ball rolling, and I want to thank him as well.

I owe a big thanks to Phil Lerman, for helping me figure out how to tell our story. And I also have to thank Brenda Copeland at St. Martin's Press, both for believing that this story was worth telling, and for her good ideas on how to make sense of it all. Thanks also to Laura Chasen at St. Martin's.

Thanks to Roger Wagner, for talking me into working on the Ballard project. If it hadn't been for you, I wouldn't have been there in the first place. Thanks also to Eddie Plana and Ed Anonical, for your help with Edith.

I want to thank my mom and dad, for making me who I am. None of this would have happened if you hadn't taught me what's important. Mom, you set the example. I was just following your lead.

More than anything, I want to thank my family, Evie, Kelsey, and Willy, for their incredible support through the years I was taking care of Edith. I missed a lot of days and nights with you guys, but you never gave me a hard time for it. I don't know how I got so lucky, but I never forget how lucky I am.

And, of course, I have to thank Edith. I want you to know I tried to tell this story—your story—as best as I could. I'm not a writer like you were and I'm sure I messed up a lot of things, and I can just hear you complaining about them already. But I got our story down as best as I could remember it. So thanks, Edith, for letting me slide a little bit. And thanks, of course, for a million other things, too.

Thank you, Edith. For all your lessons.
For all your stories.
And for changing my life.